Woodland Watercolor

A coloring workbook

Clare Therese Gray

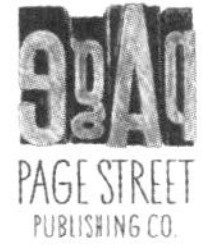
PAGE STREET
PUBLISHING CO.

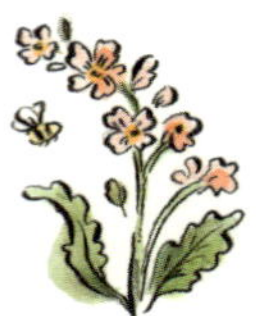

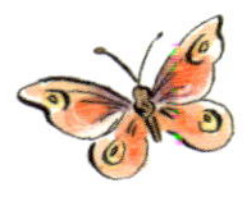

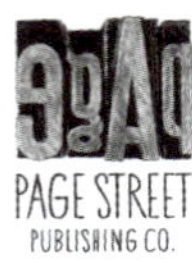

First published in 2023 by
Page Street Publishing Co.
27 Congress Street, Suite 1511
Salem, MA 01970
www.pagestreetpublishing.com

Distributed by Macmillan, sales in Canada by The Canadian Manda Group.

29   28   27   26   5 6 7 8

ISBN-13: 978-1-64567-611-9
ISBN-10: 1-64567-611-0

Cover and book illustrations © Clare Gray

Printed and bound in China

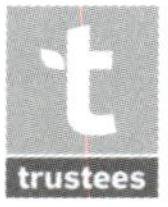

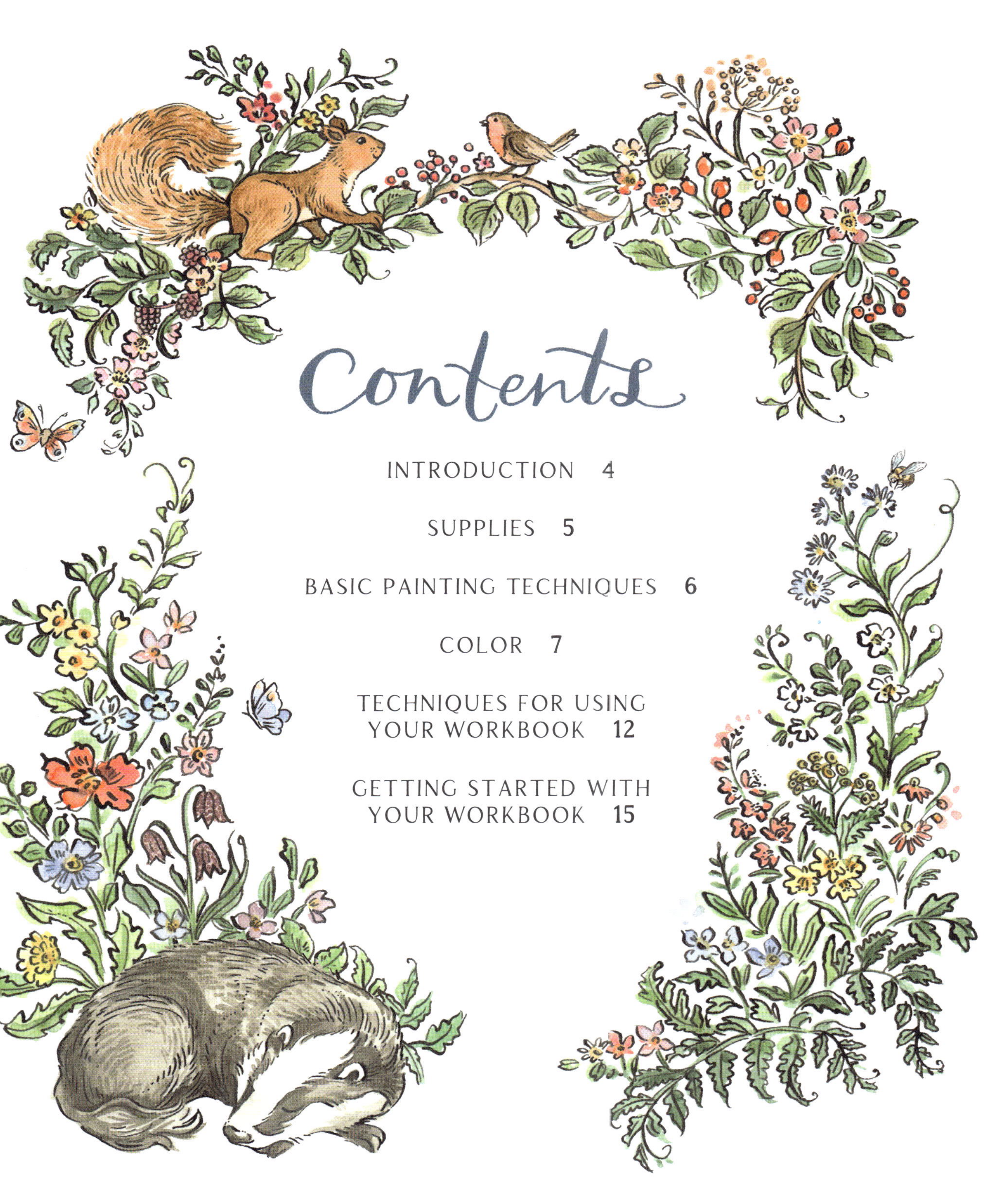

Contents

Introduction

Hello and welcome to *Woodland Watercolor*, a fresh approach to coloring using watercolor paint and paper! I have long imagined creating a coloring book that combined my love of the natural world with pen-and-ink drawings, one that could also be used as a workbook to help artists develop their personal practice.

Coloring can be wonderfully relaxing, and these 40 projects weave through the seasons so you can bring an expansive array of flora and fauna to life with color. This is a space for you to unleash your creativity, creating 40 vibrant ink-and-wash effect artworks.

This introduction guides you through the basics of working with watercolor, including paint handling, color selection and mixing, but it also explains some handy techniques. With this workbook, we can experiment with new media, such as watercolor pencils and masking fluid. We can color a whole woodland world from treetop squirrels to swimming otters to bluebell woods!

I'd love to see how you're getting on! Find me on Instagram @claretheresegray, and share your journey with the hashtag #colorwithclare.

Clare

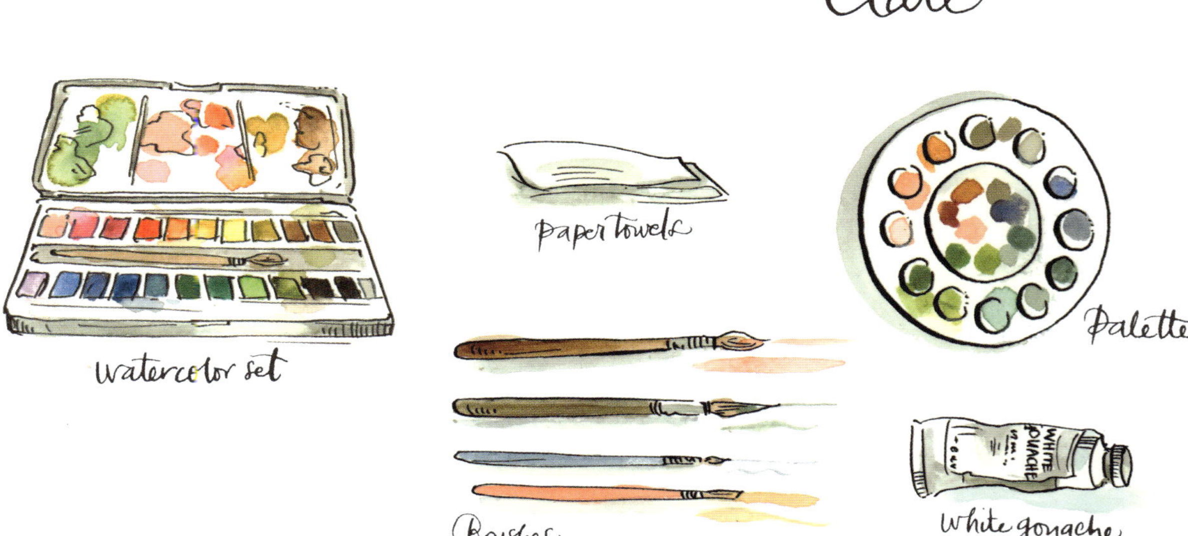

Supplies

- **Watercolor set:** Watercolors come in two sizes: a full or half pan (with little rectangular "cakes" of dry paint), and they usually come with 12, 24 or 48+ colors. Watercolor also comes in tubes of wet paint that you can squeeze into empty pans and then leave to dry to create your own unique set. Which set you decide to use is a personal choice, but the more the merrier, I say.

- **Brushes**: A set of round watercolor brushes sizes 0 through 5 work best for these projects; it is also helpful to have a fine brush or two in sizes 0 to 000. I also find a very small, angled brush useful.

- **Paper towels:** These are helpful for blotting and cleaning brushes.

- **Applicators:** You can use a fine synthetic brush, dip pen or ruling pen, but everyday items such as toothpicks or toothbrushes can be handy as well!

- **White gouache:** A small 0.5-fluid-ounce (14-ml) tube will do the job.

- **Sketchbook/watercolor paper pad:** The paper in this book is 200 gsm watercolor art paper, which is of a medium weight and means that you can add some (but not a lot of) water to the page before it starts wrinkling up. You may find it useful to have an additional pad of watercolor paper for practice swatches and experiments with color and brushstrokes.

- **Water jars:** Clean jars of water are essential for fresh, bright color. Change the water often, definitely before it gets murky, and always remember to wipe down the edges of the jars too!

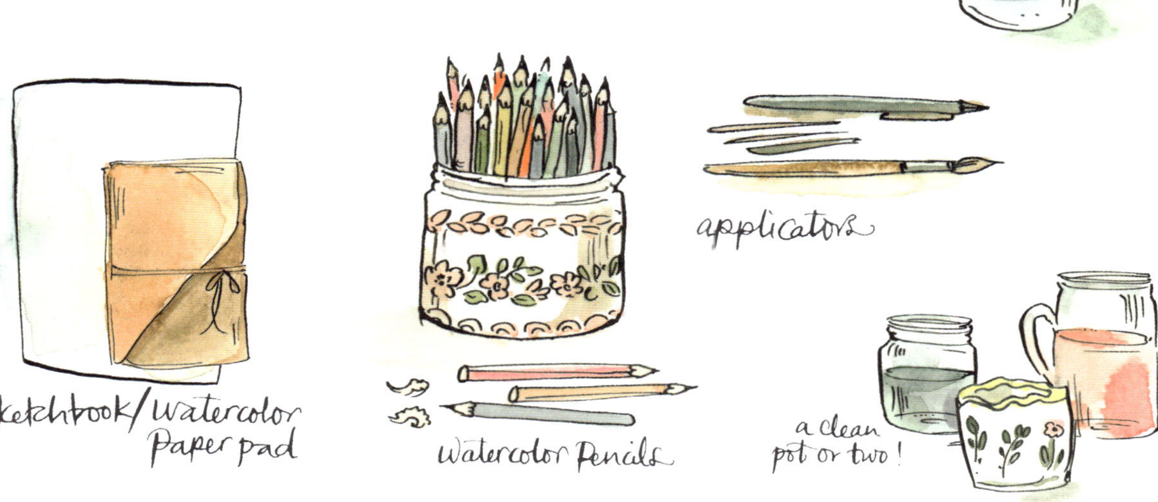

Basic Painting Techniques

Before we begin, it's important to understand a few basic watercolor techniques. To start with, your brush should always be wet. Start by gently swilling it in your clean water jar, then dab it on the rim a couple of times to remove excess water. The bristles should be fluid but not beading or dripping.

Watercolor paint is highly pigmented, and you only need a small amount to create a vibrant shade. The more water you add to the dab of pigment, the more diluted the color will be on the page. Using less water will result in a more intense and vibrant color.

Try playing around with dabs of pure color and adding varying amounts of water to your watercolor paper pad to get a feel for your chosen brush and color. I would recommend doing this with all the colors in your set, as their true shades will appear very different on paper compared to the dry pan.

Here are four basic techniques you may find useful when painting in your workbook:

WET ON DRY

"Wet on dry" simply means you're applying wet paint to a dry surface or a painted page that has fully dried.

WET ON WET

"Wet on wet" means you're adding wet paint to an already wet page, causing the paint to bleed with a diffused edge. This can be useful when blending, but be careful not to soak your workbook pages too much, as color may seep through to the reverse of the page.

LAYERING

"Layering" is a wet-on-dry technique. With watercolor, it is important to start with lighter layers of color and wait until they are completely dry before adding another layer. Once dry, richer color and intensity can be achieved by adding additional layers. The more layers, the darker and more intense the color will be.

BLENDING

"Blending" is both a wet-on-wet and wet-on-dry technique. Two colors can be blended directly onto your piece; once both colors are added side by side on the page, you can merge the two using a damp brush. Alternatively, you can paint different colored layers on top of already-dry layers and lightly combine them. However, I would recommend mixing the colors in your palette rather than directly on the page so you can subtly build up intensity.

Color

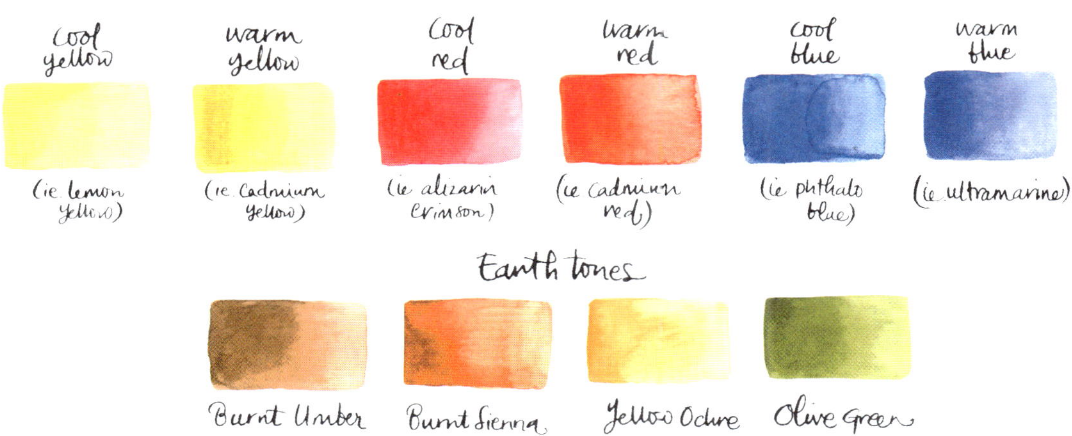

You are able to mix a beautiful range of colors with even a small watercolor set. Most sets will contain two of each of the primary colors: red, yellow and blue. One will be "warm" and one "cool." "Warm" simply means that they have a yellow, red or orange hue, and "cool" colors tend to have a blue, green or purple tint. There will also be some useful earth tones—which are warm colors with brown hues, such as burnt sienna, burnt umber and yellow ochre—as well as a white, which you can use to create pastel shades.

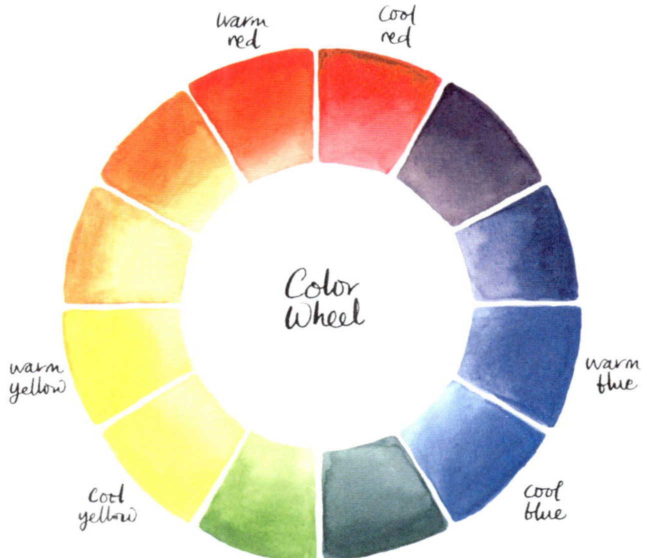

COLOR MIXING

This color wheel gives a simple visual explanation of how to mix an array of colors to produce countless new colors for your projects.

Complementary colors sit opposite each other on the wheel, such as pink and green or blue and orange. They may appear jarring at first glance, but when they are used subtly, they can create wonderfully surprising combinations.

BLACK

Black should be used very sparingly to avoid creating a muddy palette (and lifeless color)! Most sets will not include black, but you can easily mix your own soft dark shade. You can do this in countless variations, but generally speaking adding all three primary colors together creates a very dark paint. Adding small amounts of black to other colors creates a darker shade of those colors.

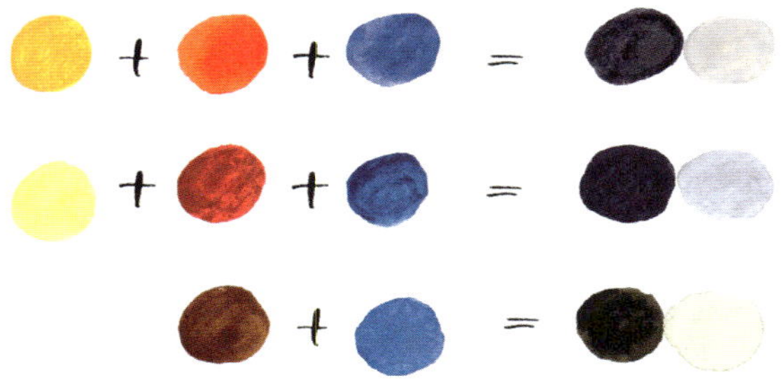

WHITE: MASKING FLUID AND WHITE GOUACHE

Your use of white is something to be considered before you begin painting. With watercolor, the only way to maintain a light area in your work is by keeping your chosen area free of paint—in other words, using the white of the page as your "white."

One way of keeping this brightness is to use masking fluid or drawing gum. This is a liquid latex–based solution that resists watercolor once it is dried. To use masking fluid, you paint it onto areas you would like to keep white (it's often tinted blue so you can see what you are doing), and then let the area dry per the instructions on the product. Once it is dry, you can continue working on your piece as normal. When the paint is dry, simply rub off the masking fluid with an eraser or finger and the original white of the page will be revealed! Only apply masking fluid to completely dry paper, otherwise you run the risk of it penetrating the top layer of the paper. This can tear or rip the paper when you remove the masking fluid.

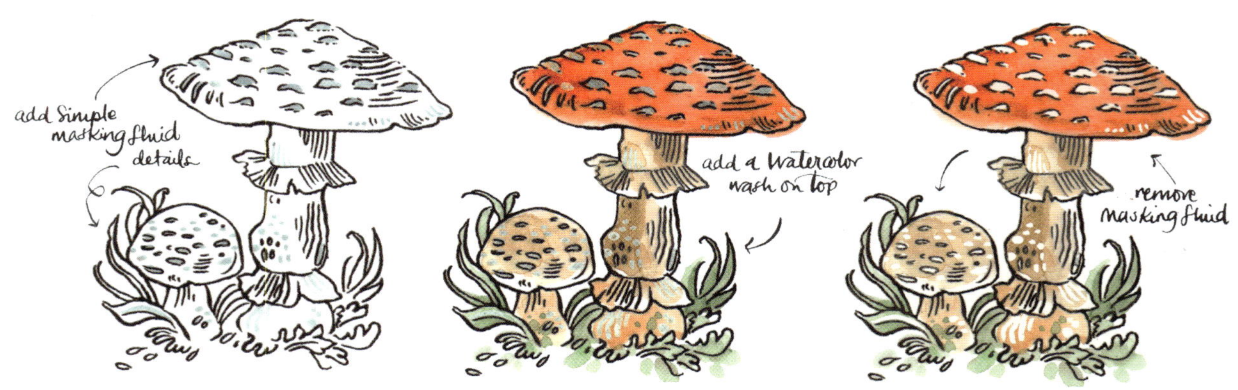

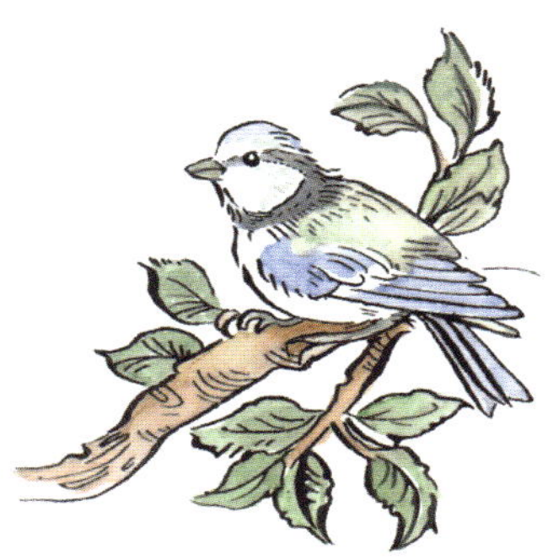

Begin with a light wash

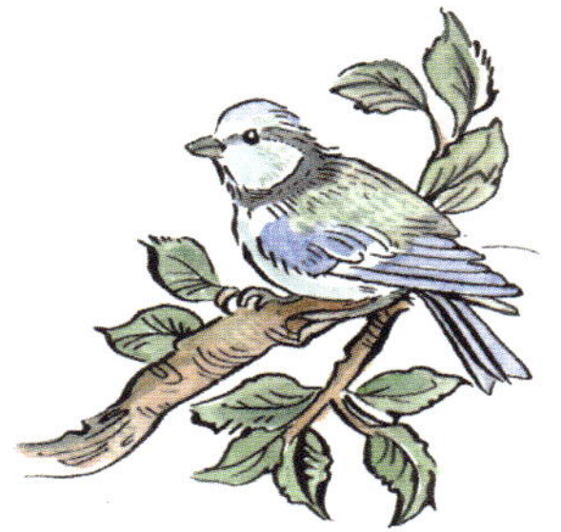

add masking fluid to areas you would like to remain light

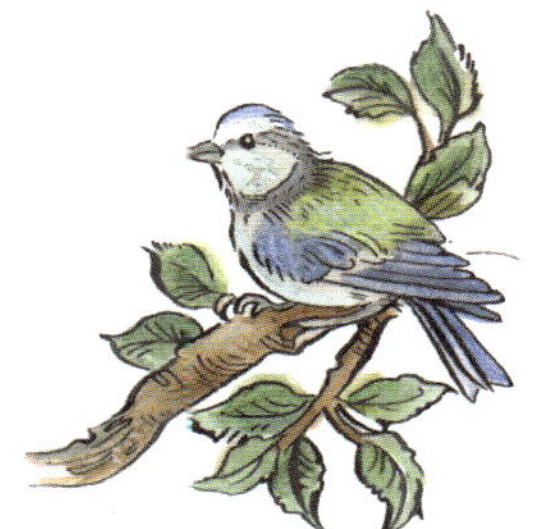

Paint another darker layer

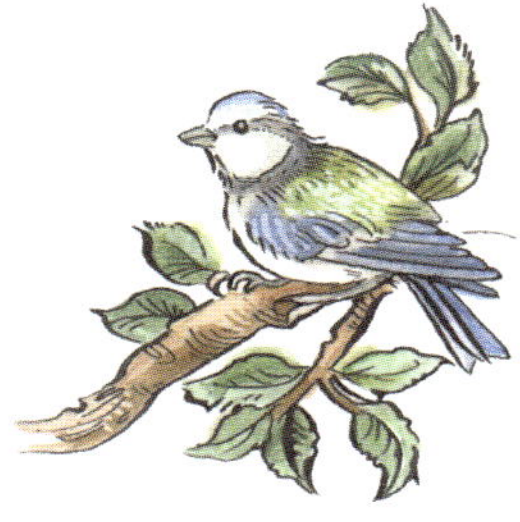

remove the masking fluid

You can apply masking fluid with an old brush or other tools, such as a clean dip pen or ruling pen. Masking fluid dries extremely quickly, so be sure to have a clean pot of water to wash your brush immediately after application or the bristles will stick together, rendering the brush useless!

Examples of where masking fluid could be useful include light on water, white spots on toadstools, cottage smoke, feathered details or highlights on berries.

It is also very effective to add masking fluid to an already painted area to create depth.

You can also use white gouache to add light high-lights. Gouache is an opaque, water-based paint, and it comes in tubes as opposed to pans. A small blob can be thinned with a little water to the consistency of watercolor and even mixed with watercolor paints to create semi-opaque pastel shades.

To keep areas of white fresh and bright, I would recommend using masking fluid in the first instance and keeping gouache in your emergency reserve!

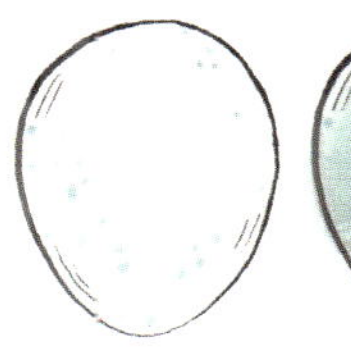
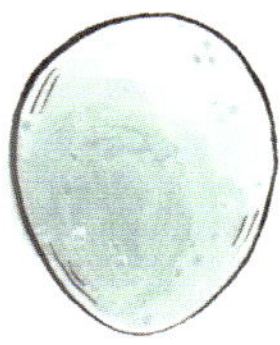
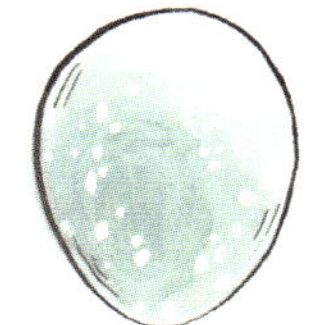

a. masking fluid speckles with watercolor on top

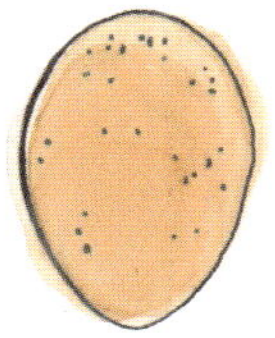
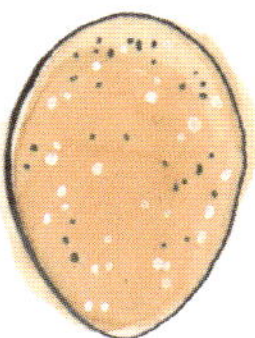

b. a watercolor wash with white gouache speckles

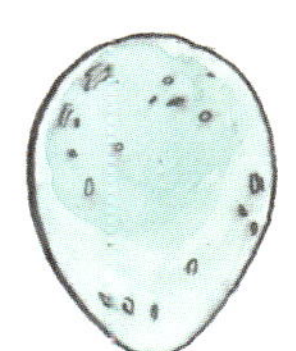
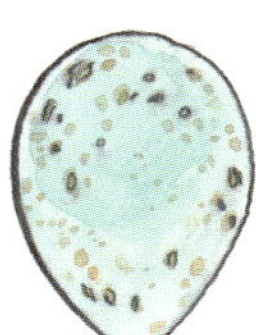
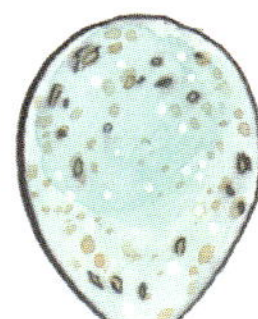

c. layers of watercolor and gouache

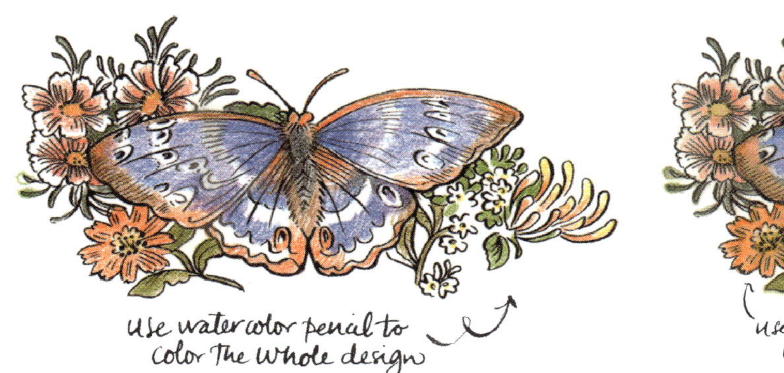

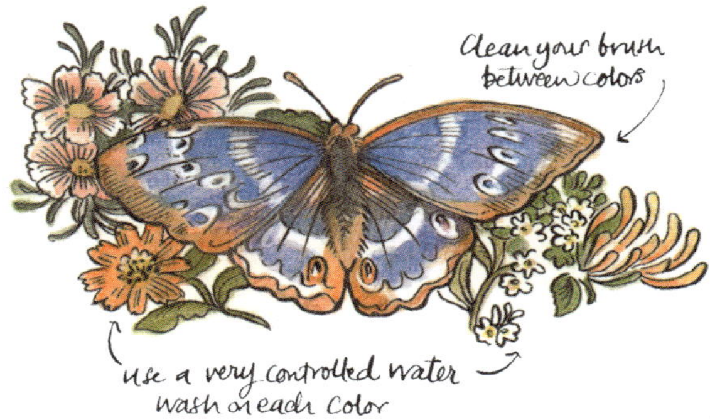

WATERCOLOR PENCILS

These are a very useful addition to your kit, although they are not strictly necessary. Watercolor pencils complement watercolor paint, and they have the bonus of being easier to control, especially with fine details. Watercolor pencils can be used in a couple of ways:

1. Color your page with the pencil and then use a wash of water to blend and create a paint-like washy effect.

2. Use watercolor pencils to add details to your watercolor paintings. This can be done in a couple of ways: wet or dry. If you draw with watercolor pencils directly onto a damp or wet page, the pigment can be very bright and rich but also difficult to remove. If you draw on dry paper, you can create a variety of layers and intensity of color by adding a little water wash. Bear in mind that your paper will be weaker when wet, and drawing on top may add texture to the surface of the paper or even create holes! (Watch out if your favorite page is on the reverse of the one you are working on!)

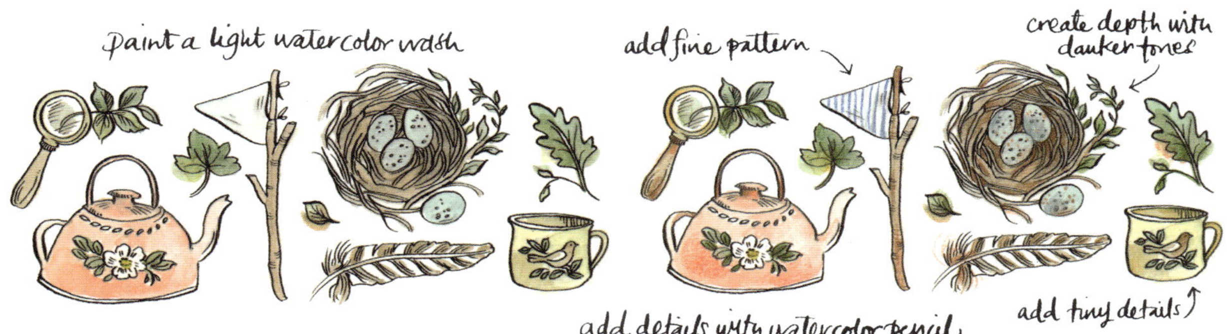

CHOOSING YOUR COLOR

So now it's time to go for it—but I hear you asking: "Which colors do I choose, and how do I create a palette?"

A "palette" is simply a collection of colors that you have chosen to use for your piece. A good way to see if colors work together is by premixing them. Next, paint swatches on your plain pad to see how they look when dried before using the palette in your workbook.

BE INSPIRED BY NATURE

Nature boasts such a wonderful range of colors from which we can draw inspiration. Try asking yourself a few questions about the project you're starting to help you come to some decisions about your palette. What season and time of day do you imagine it to be? What kind of weather is it? The workbook follows the year through the seasons, and this is one way to think about an original use of color. What colors do you associate with the season? Could you use these more prominently in a piece?

RESEARCH THE WORLD AROUND YOU

What do different fungi actually look like, and how might it be fun to try and replicate the colors you find? What shades of brown and blue are real bird eggs? What does a woodland look like in moonlight? What shades of green are pine needles as opposed to oak leaves? Search for images online, or, even better, get outside and see for yourself!

TRY USING AN IMAGINATIVE PALETTE

Although the subjects of these coloring projects are relatively realistic and close to life, we absolutely do not have to try and replicate them exactly. Have you seen a beautiful palette somewhere you would like to try on one of the pages? Why not have a pink and teal wreath as opposed to a green and red one? Could a background be purple instead of a traditional dusky blue? Don't be afraid to explore your creativity.

FIND YOUR OWN COLOR IDENTITY

At the end of the day, this is your journey and workbook. Choose colors you love and that you respond to in your own and in others' work. How do certain colors make you feel? Do you have a favorite color that you enjoy using?

Round brushes are useful, as you can use both the thickness and point of the brush tip to create a variety of strokes. Experiment with the selection you have on hand on your plain paper pad to see how many different thicknesses of strokes you can make. It's very handy to have at least one fine brush for little details such as leaf veins or animal fur.

There you have a few techniques that may be helpful to consider. Flip back to this handy reference page as you find new opportunities to use them in this workbook or in other projects.

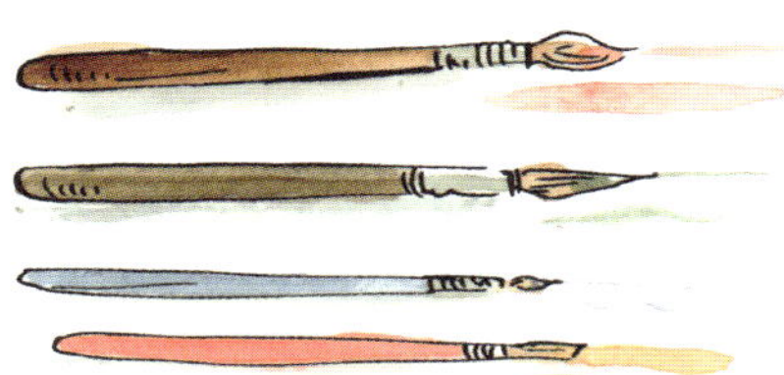

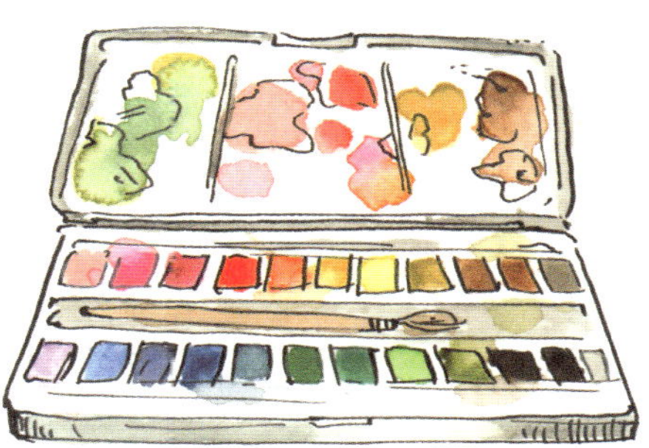

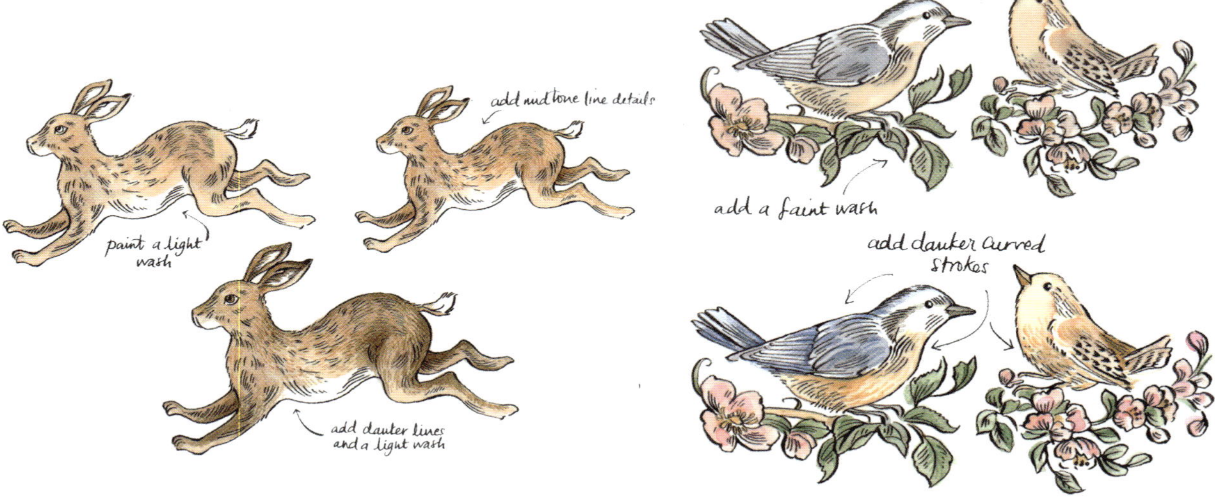

PAINTING FUR

Create texture by building soft layers of color with detailed strokes using a fine brush.

PAINTING FEATHERS

This time use curved, soft strokes to add feathered details.

PAINTING SKIES

I would recommend using a larger round or flat brush for wider skies. Before you begin, think about the time of day taking place in your project. Having a photo reference on hand may be useful when choosing color.

It may be helpful to work on the sky and clouds in steps.

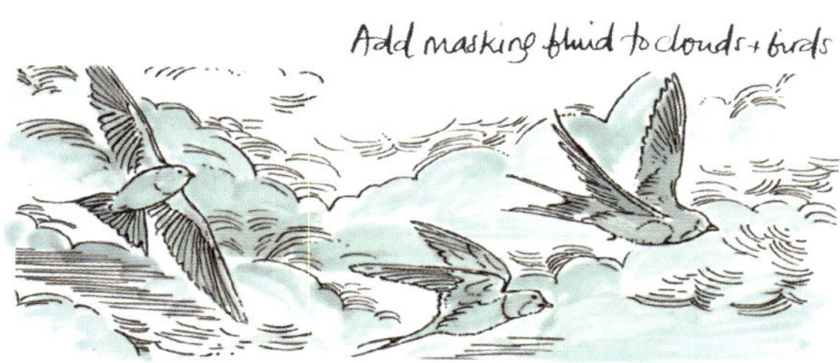

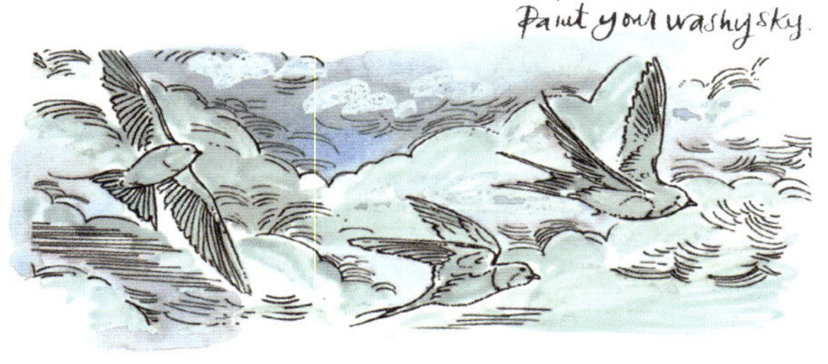

1. Begin by adding masking to areas of cloud or birds that you would like to remain white.

2. Paint watery layer(s) of paint, allowing colors to bleed and blend, then leave to dry.

3. Peel the masking fluid off, revealing white clouds.

4. Paint the birds. Think about the tones of grey, blue, yellow or pink there are in real clouds, and how they're often darker at the bottom. Work in extremely light layers to build up color just in the white areas.

5. Finish by looking at the sky as a whole; you may need some brushstrokes to tie it all together.

PAINTING LEAVES

I love using a range of colors within leaves and trees, and it can be a delight to mix and work with several greens. Try blending a couple of colors on one leaf! Layer fine details, imperfections, spots, holes and veins on top of dried color to add intriguing and realistic details.

Experiment using this basic diagram to create a range of greens, and see what happens when you add more water.

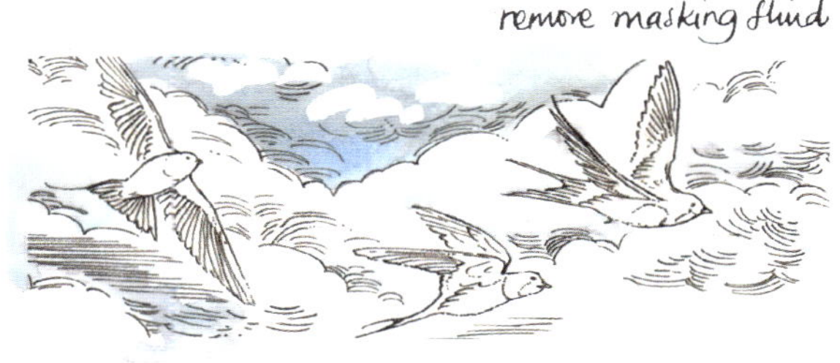

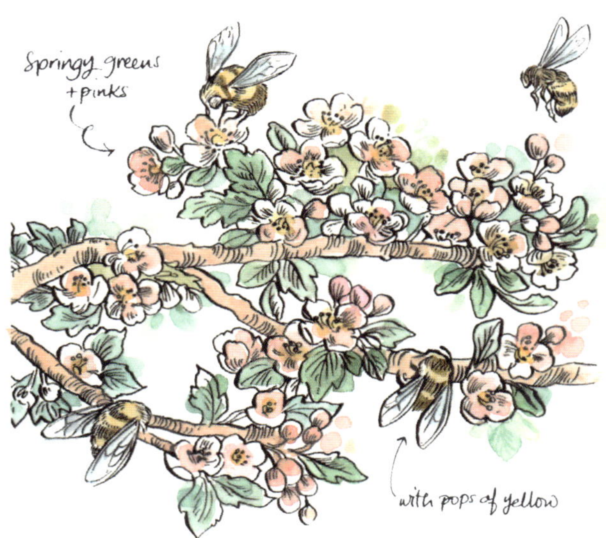

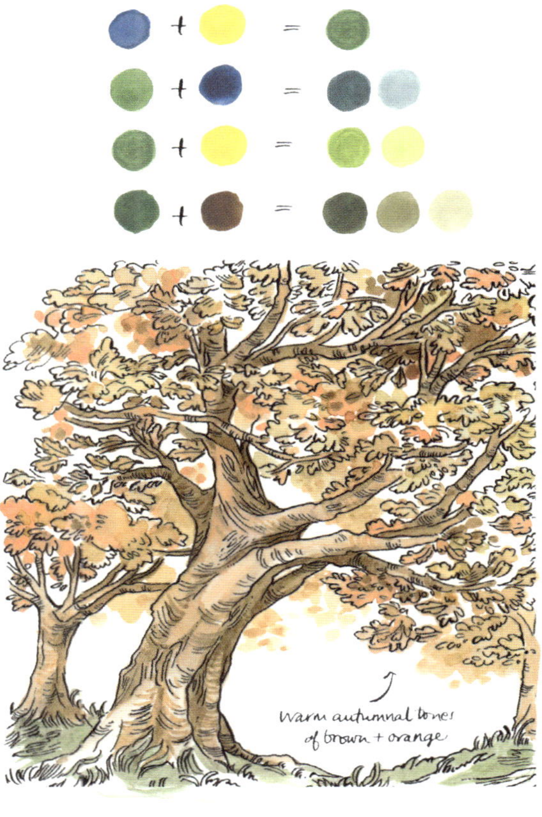

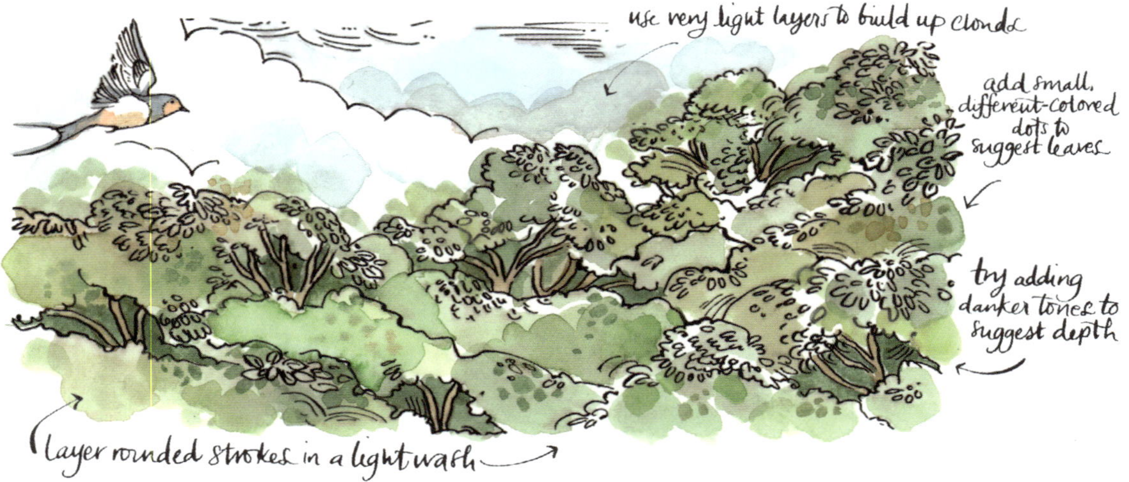

ADDING DETAILS OUTSIDE THE LINES

One of the joys of working with ink-and-wash drawings is the opportunity to splash about. You don't have to only paint inside lines. Use these examples to inspire your work.

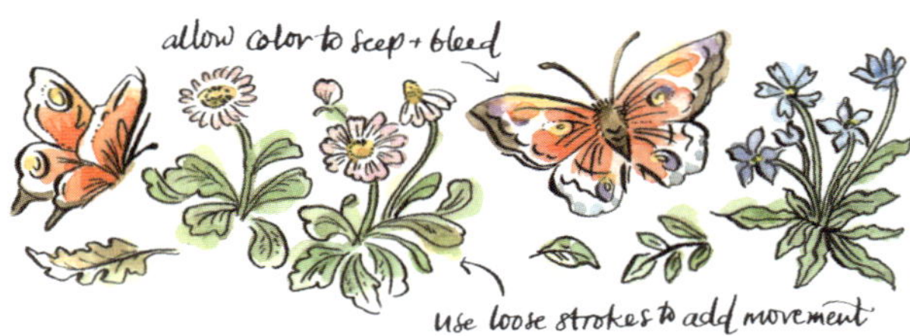

Getting Started With Your Workbook

Your workbook is your own personal place to explore and experiment with watercolor. Take care of your book so you can enjoy coloring every page!

The paper in this book is 200 gsm, the heaviest grade watercolor paper available for publishing. While this may not handle as much water as you may be used to with conventional watercolor paper, it is still very robust and its beautiful surface is perfect for coloring intricate details. Have paper towels on hand while you paint so you can easily blot excess water.

With this in mind, if you would like your page to dry flat to frame, I would advise very carefully slicing the page out of your workbook with a penknife. Next, tape the edges to a board (with low tack tape) so that when it dries, the image remains perfectly flat!

This workbook is bound on one side, so before you begin, you will need to flatten down your chosen page as much as possible so that it sits open and flat. Also bear in mind that once you have finished, your artwork will likely be wet or damp, and you will need to keep the book propped open until it is thoroughly dried so that pages do not stick together.

Starting a fresh page can be daunting. With each project, there are a few questions you need to think about before beginning:

- Is your equipment on hand, with a couple of jars of fresh water, clean brushes and blotting tissue?

- What kind of color palette would you like to use? Have you tried mixing a few of the colors on your palette and painting swatches on paper to see how they work together?

- Are there areas you would like to keep light or white?

In my experience, the best way to dive in is to use light washes, building up color in layers with a more diluted pigment. Be patient and leave layers to dry—it's easy to build color intensity gradually, but it is nearly impossible to remove strong pigment. It won't take long for your confidence and experience with watercolor to grow. Don't stress about making mistakes—you will be able to remove some of the color by lightly dabbing clean water and removing it with fresh paper towels. Always leave your work to dry before working on top so that you don't damage the surface of the paper.

I hope this book really inspires your creativity and you enjoy painting your own watercolor woodland! No matter where you are on your artistic journey, don't forget that this is your place for exploration and experimentation.

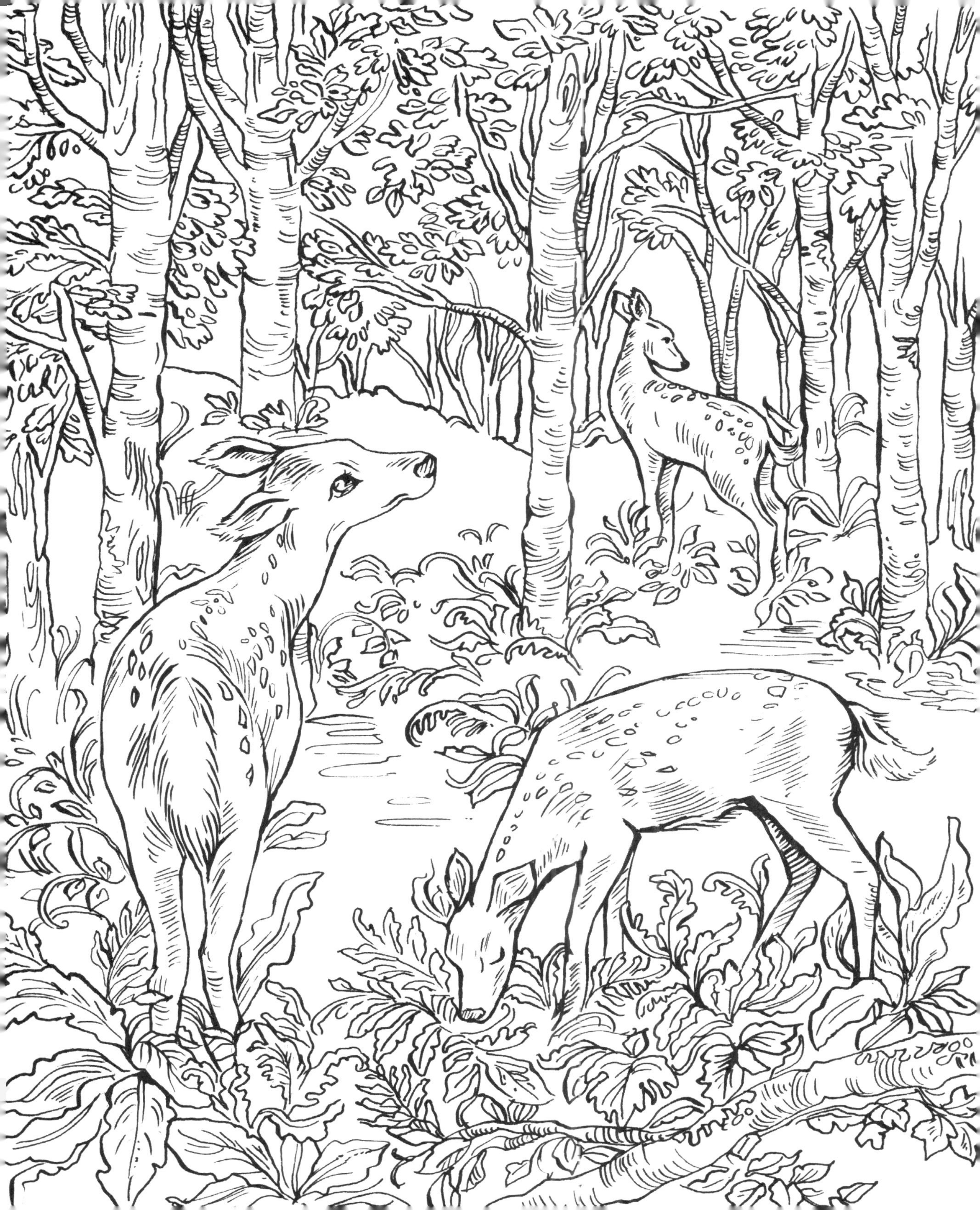

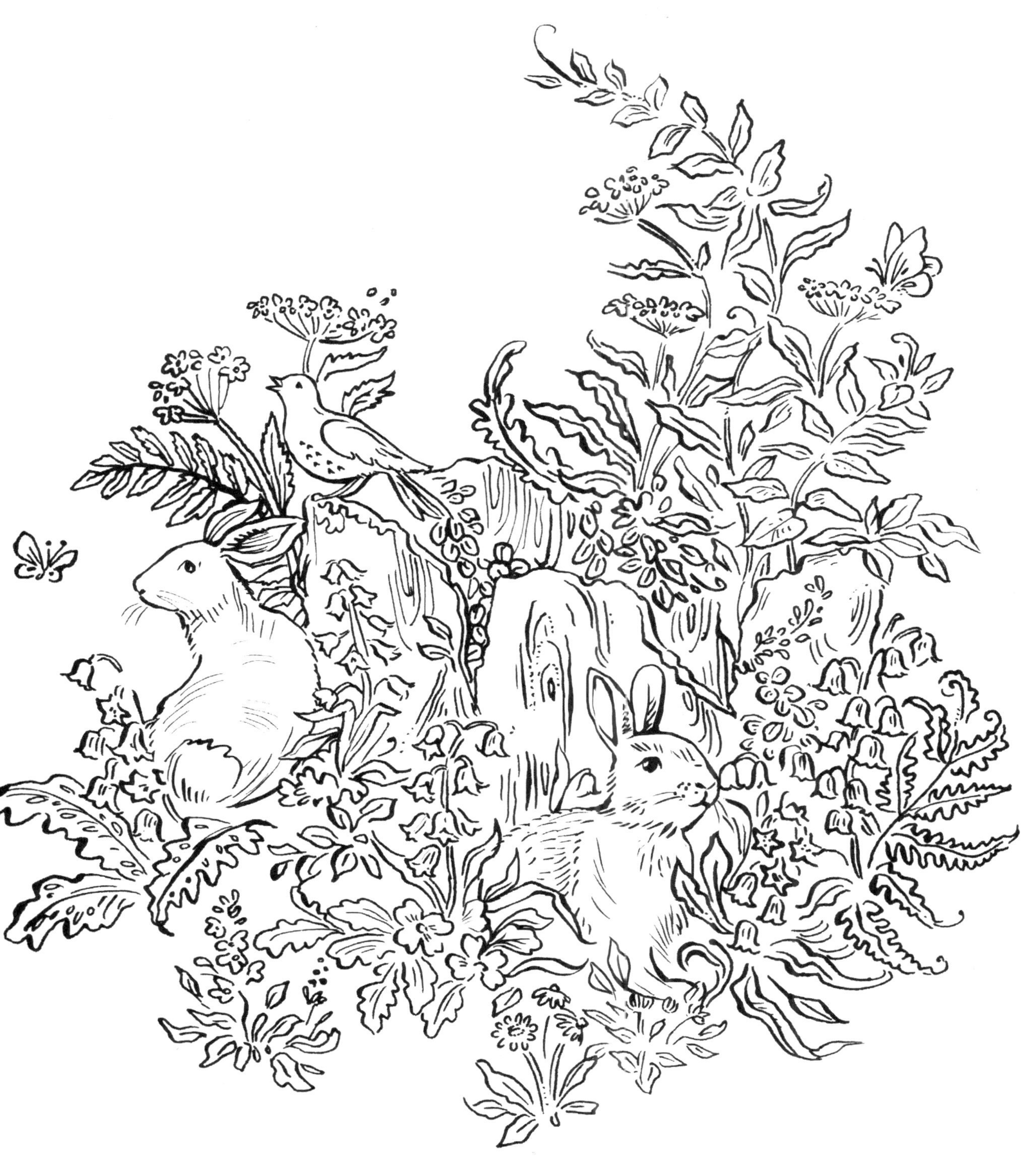

Eggs

Starling
Robin
Nuthatch
Bluebird
Song Sparrow
Crow
Nightingale
Blue Jay
Goldfinch
Oriole
Wren
Mallard
Meadowlark
Jackdaw
Blackbird
Ring-Necked Pheasant
Tree Creeper
Chaffinch
Song Thrush
Magpie

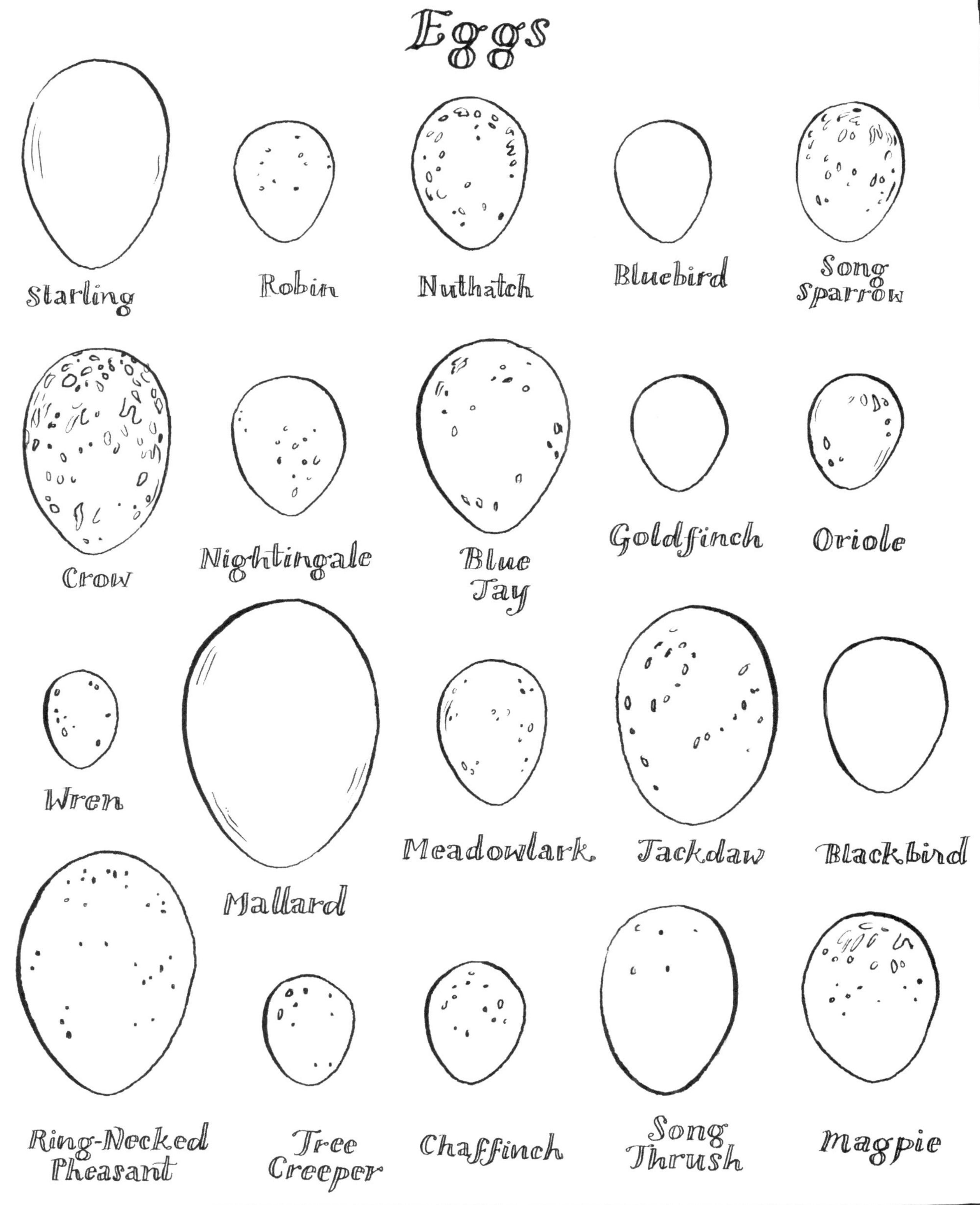

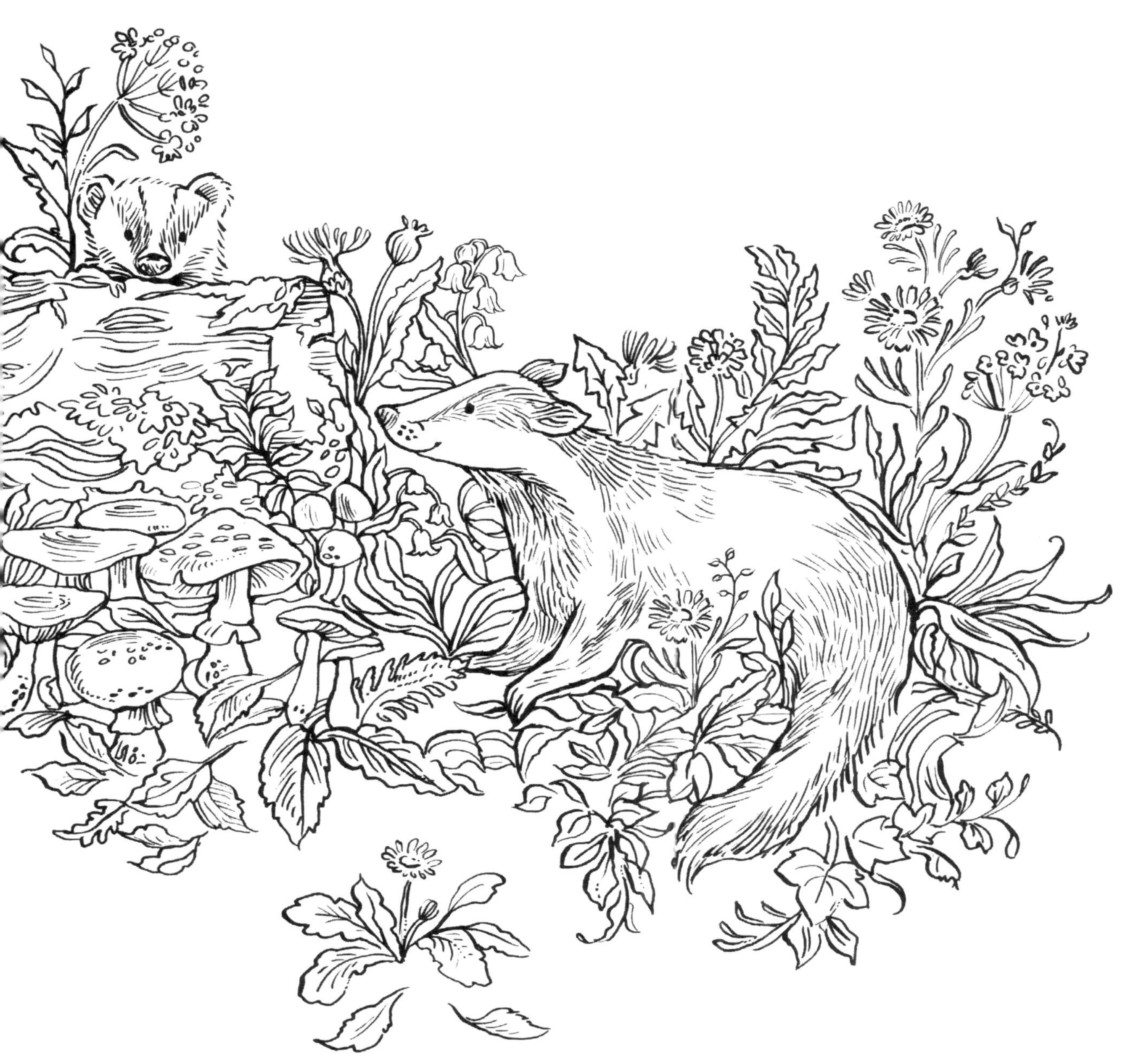

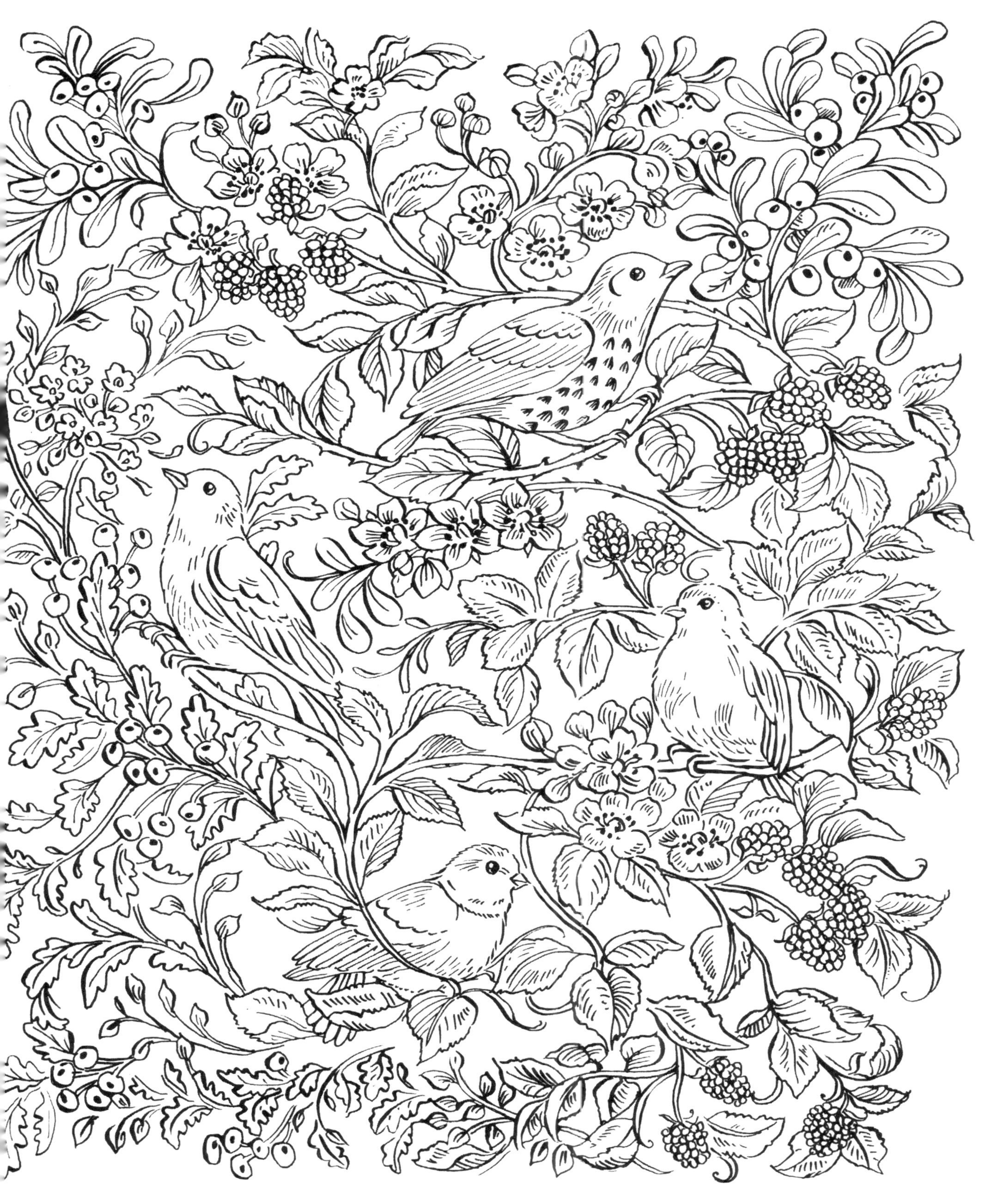

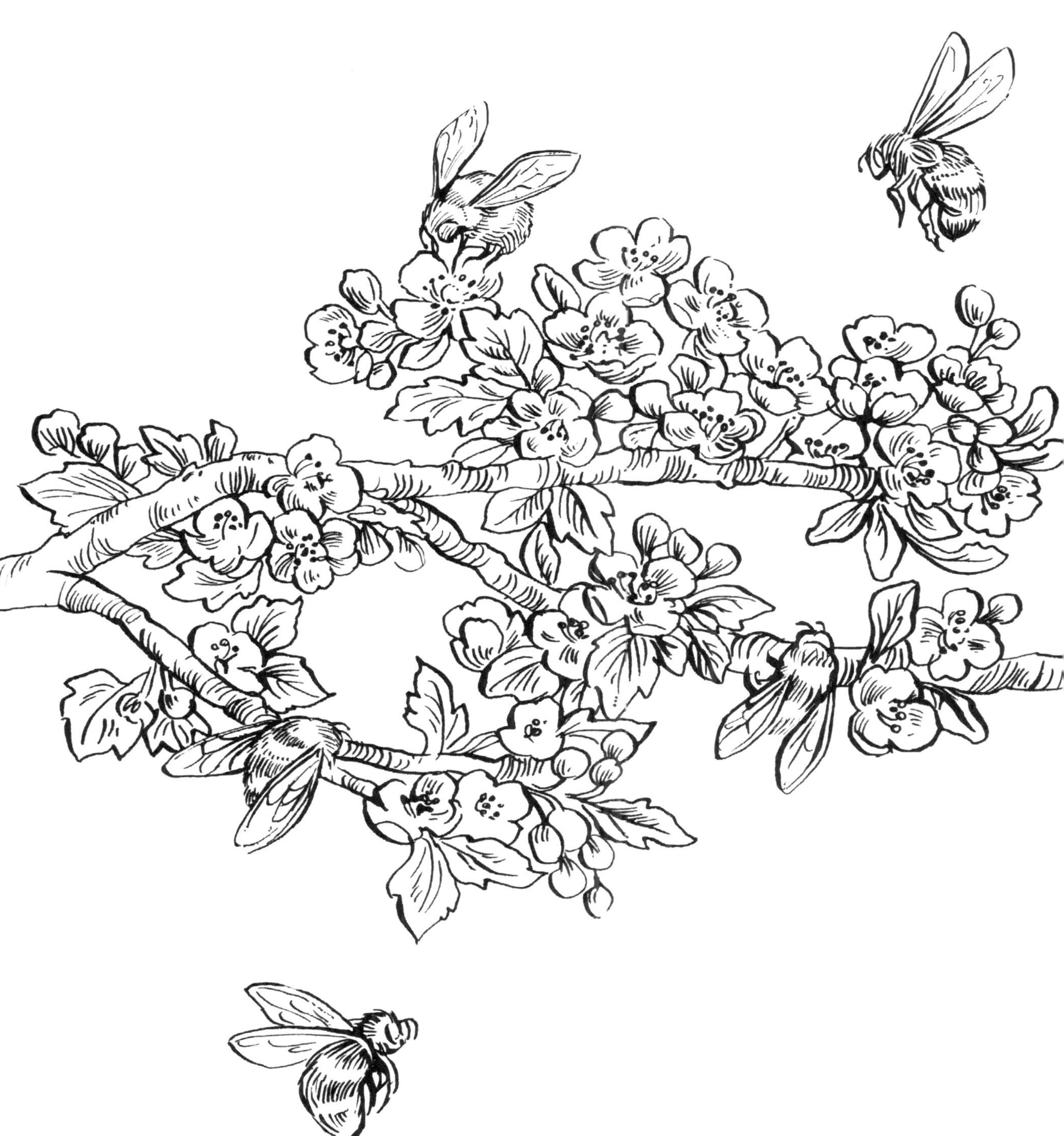

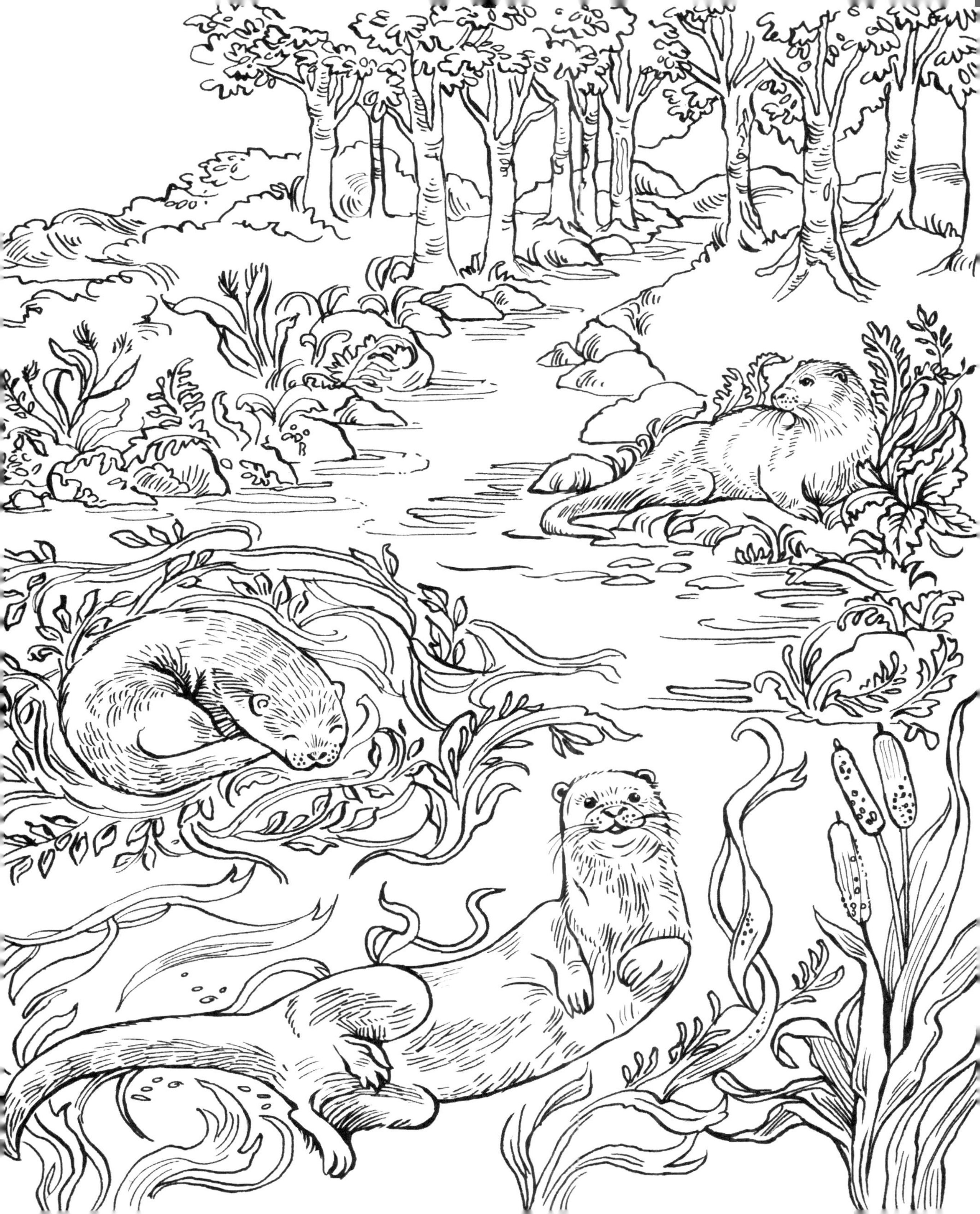

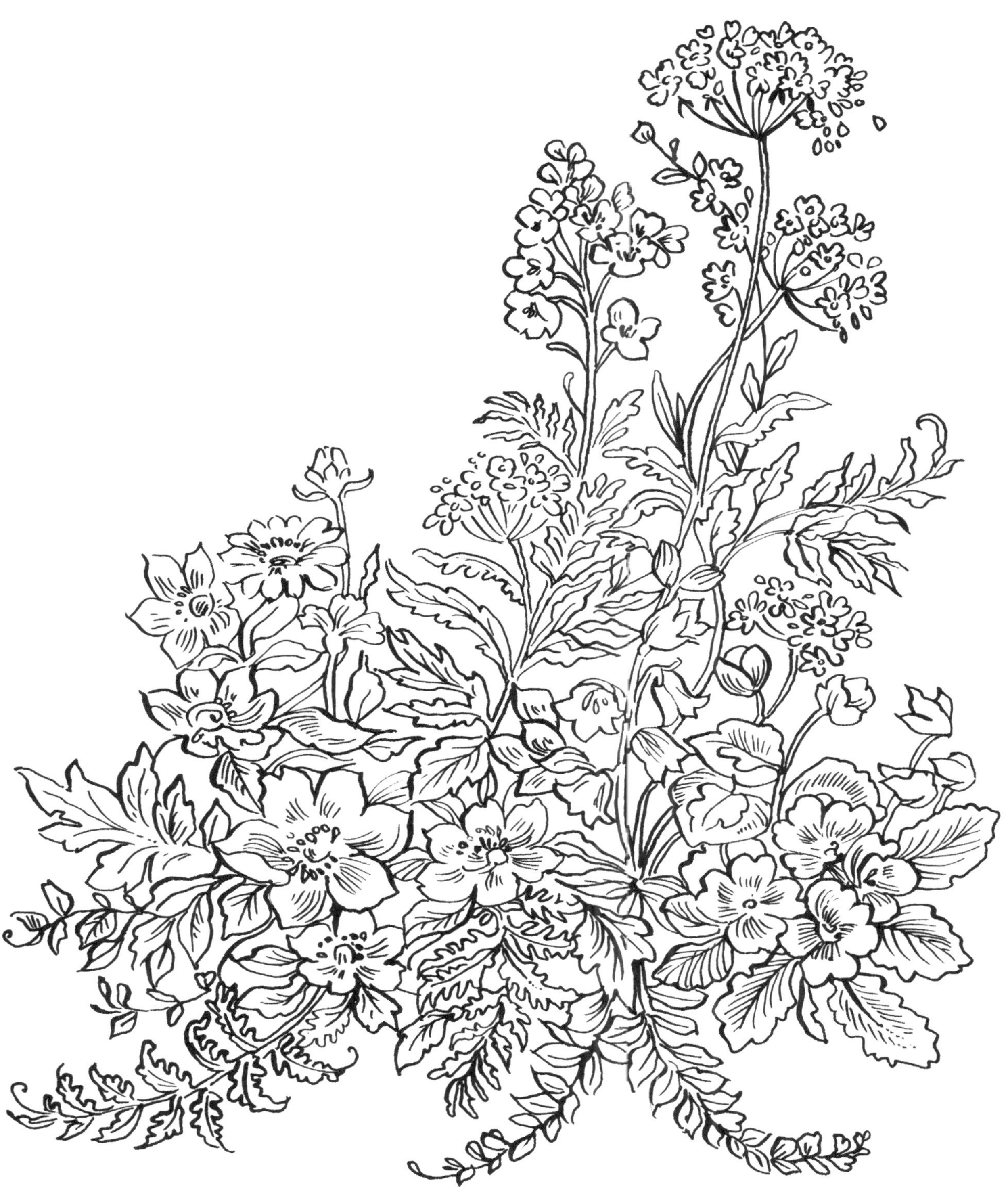

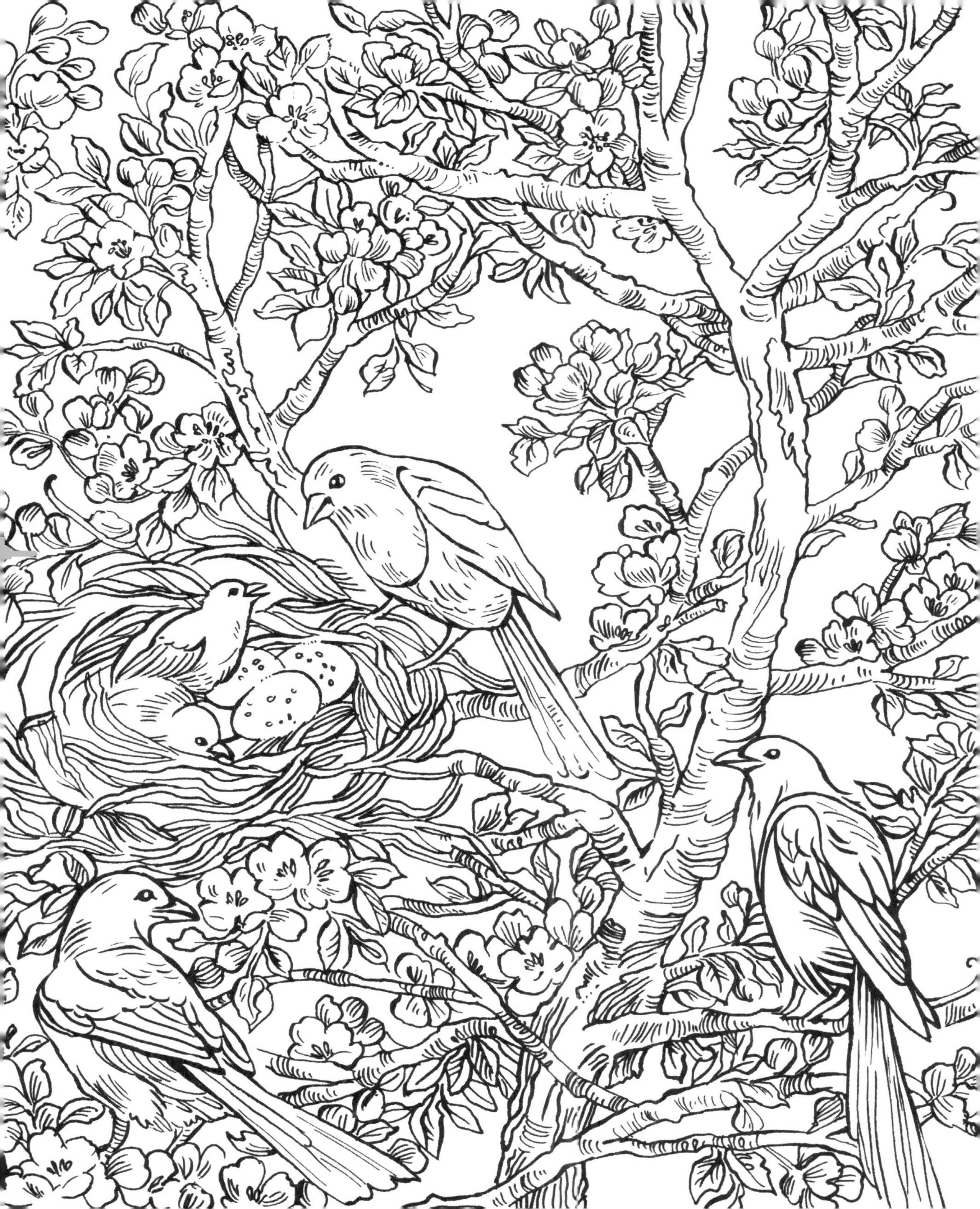

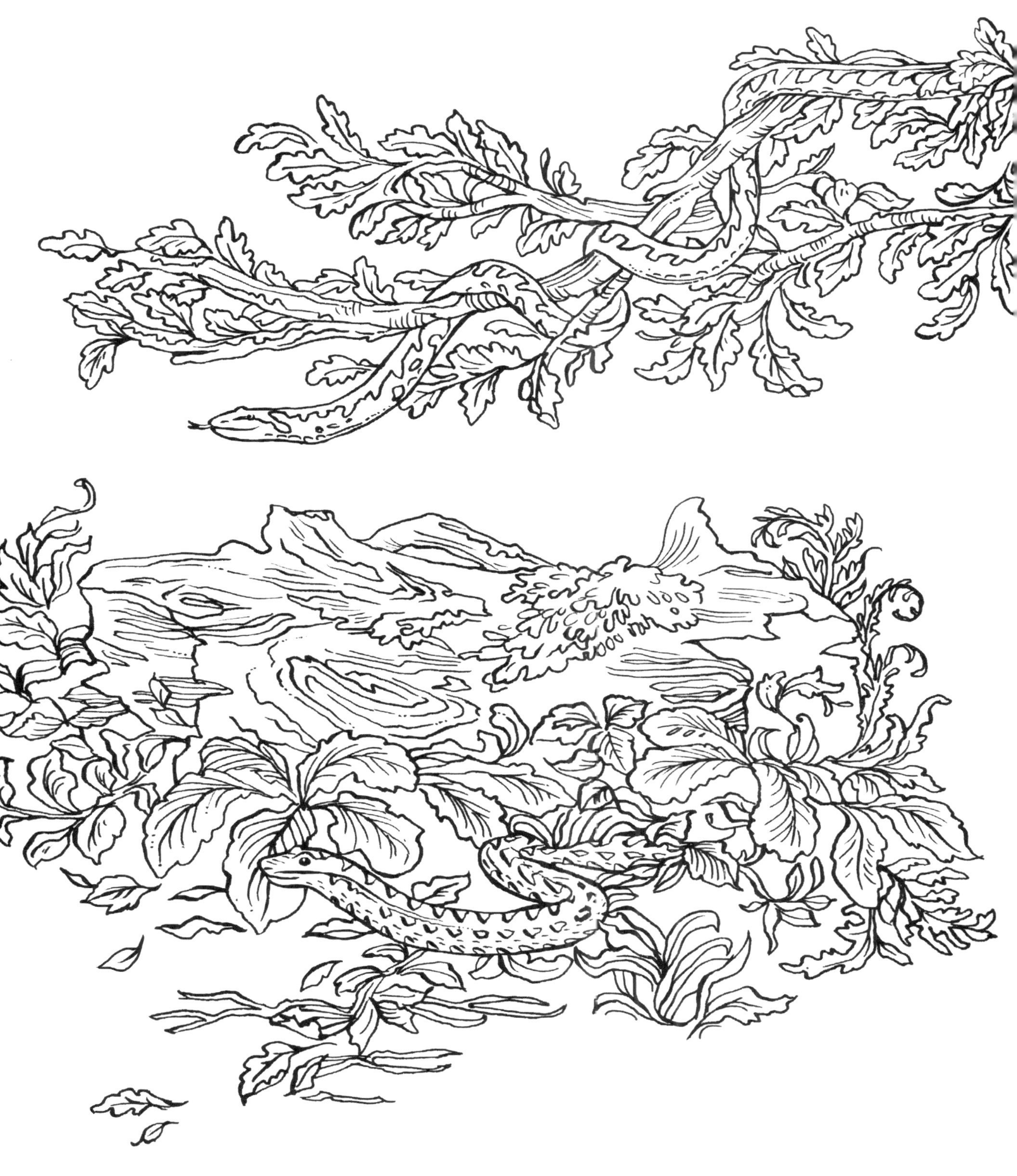

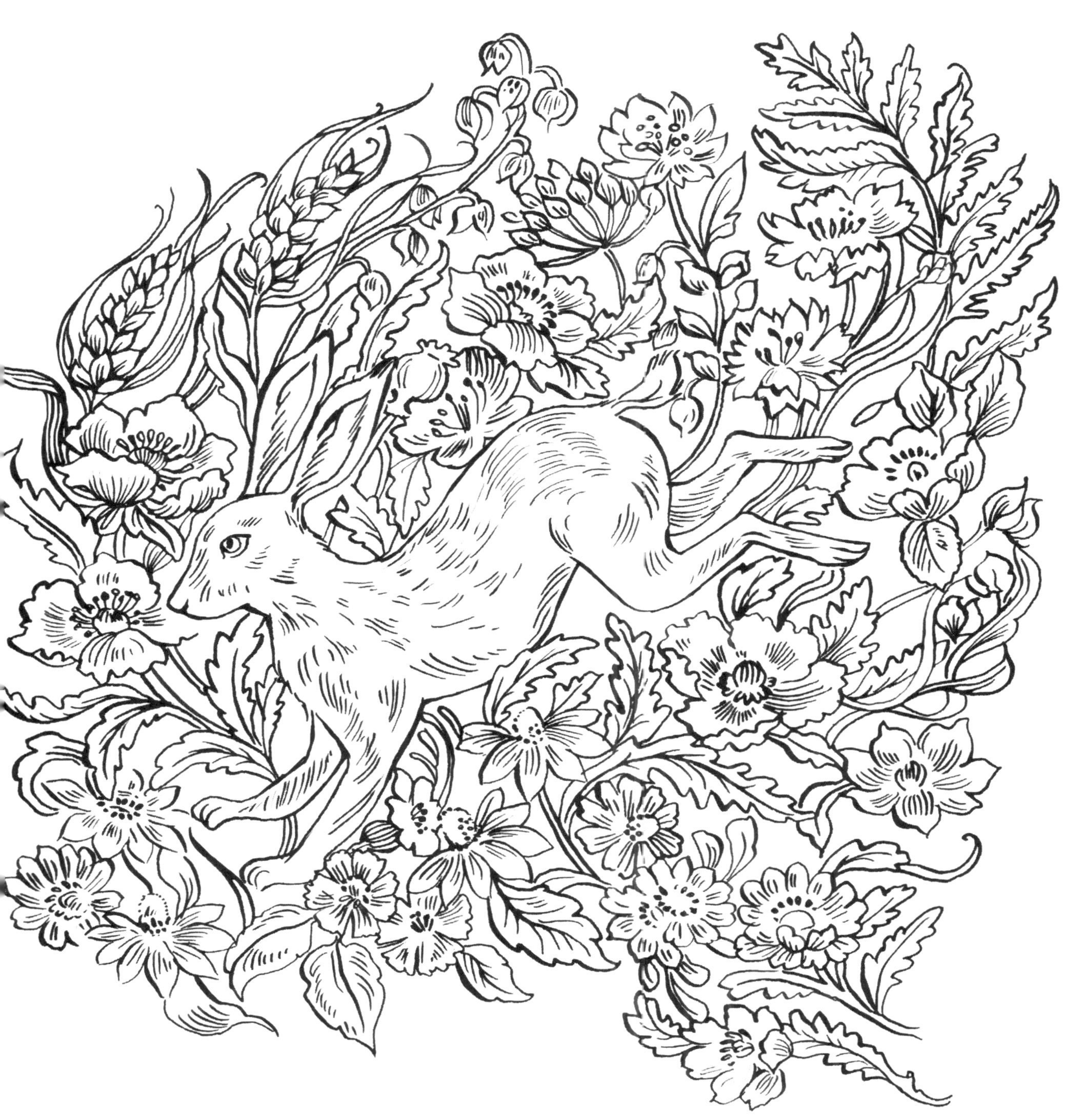

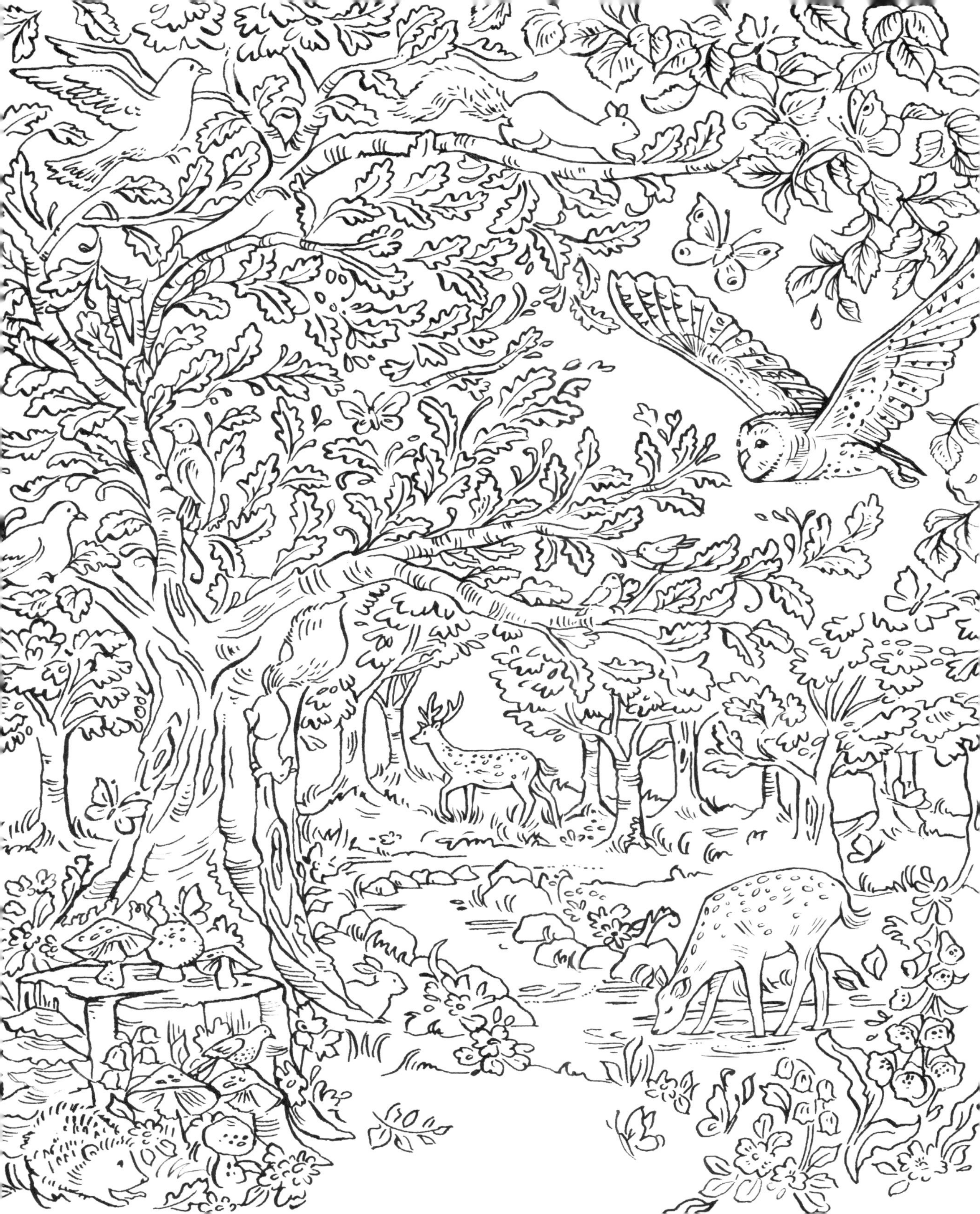

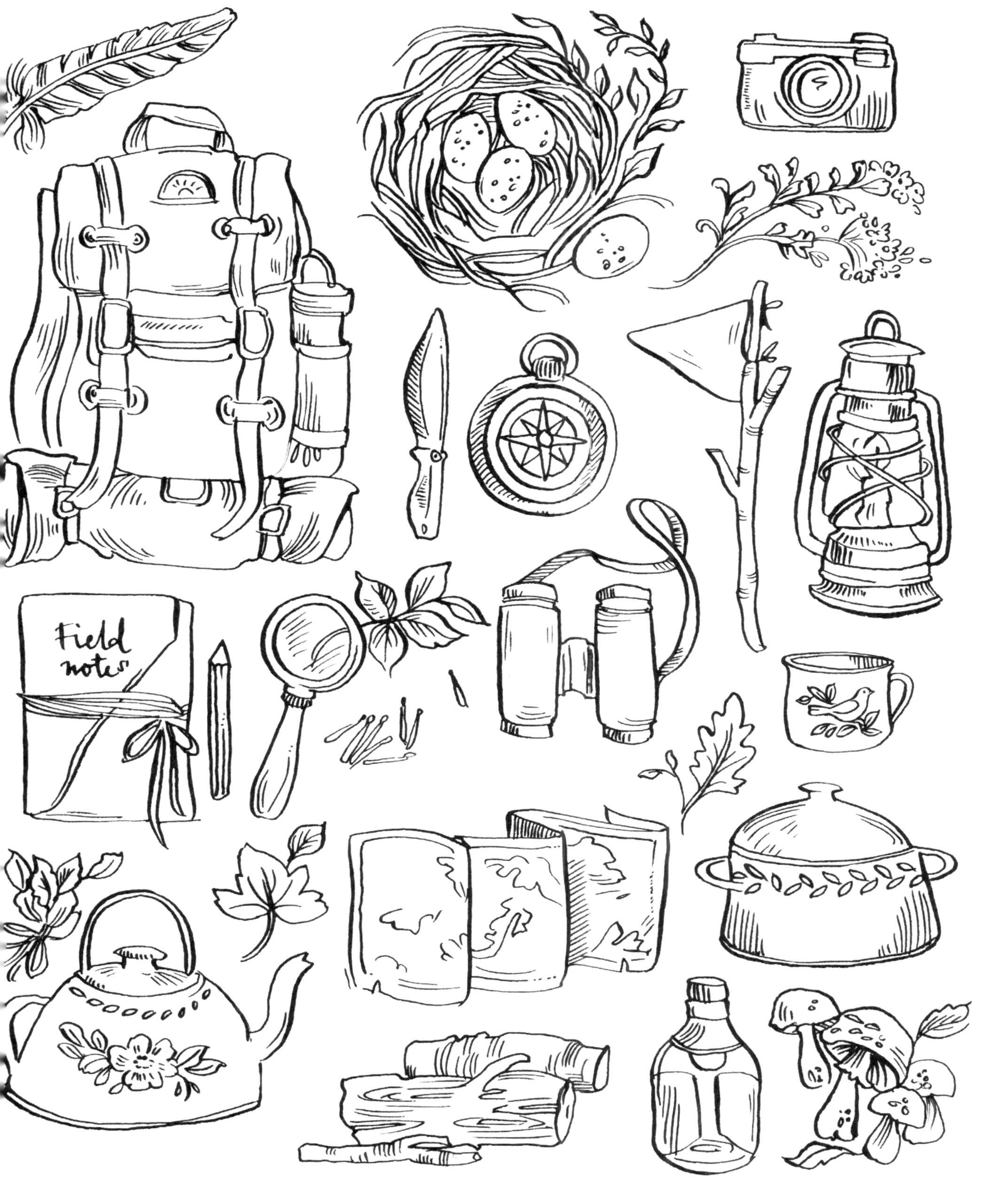

Field
notes

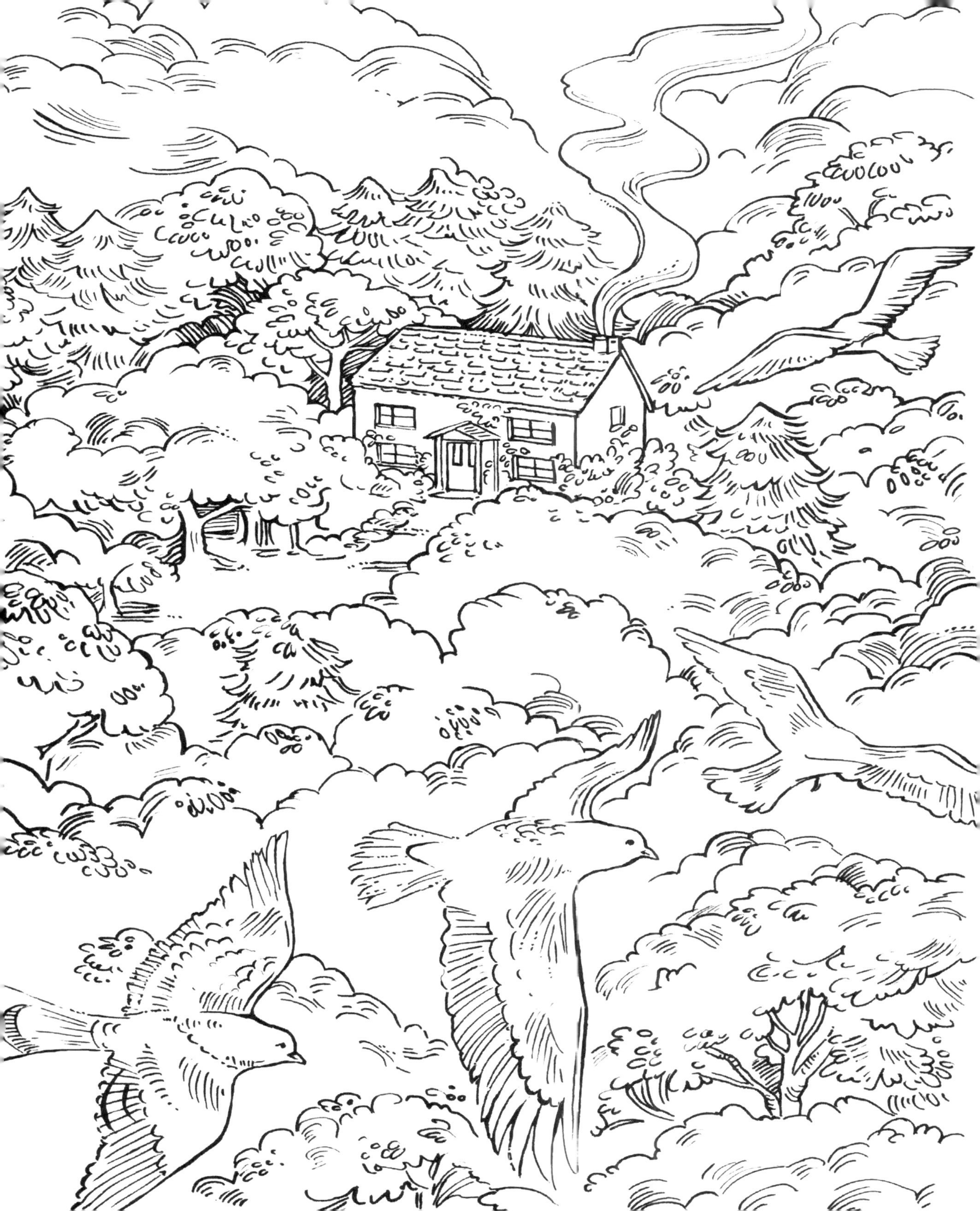

I. PRIMROSE

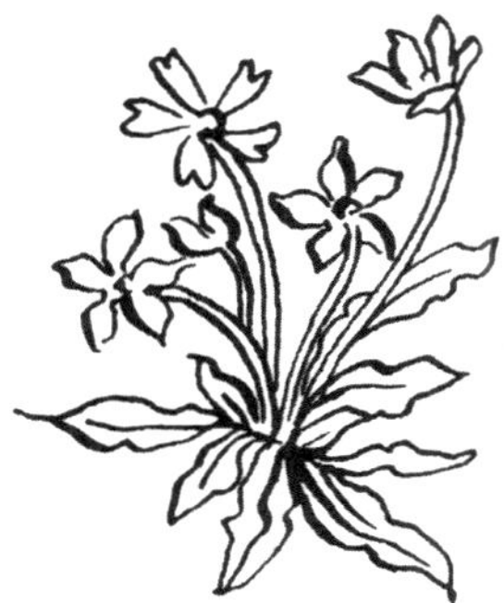

II. BLUE PHLOX

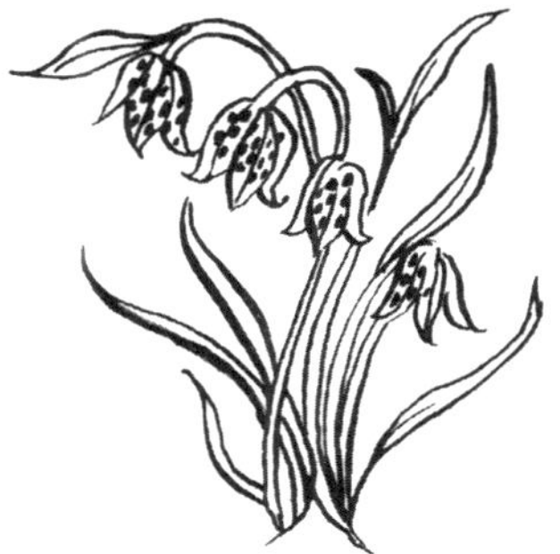

III. SNAKE'S HEAD FRITILLARY

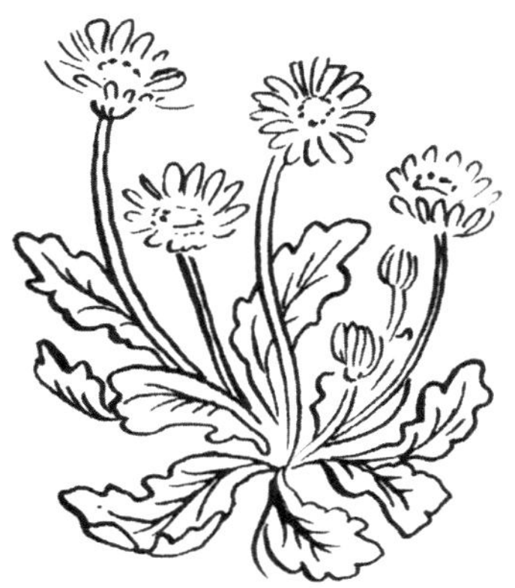

IV. DAISY

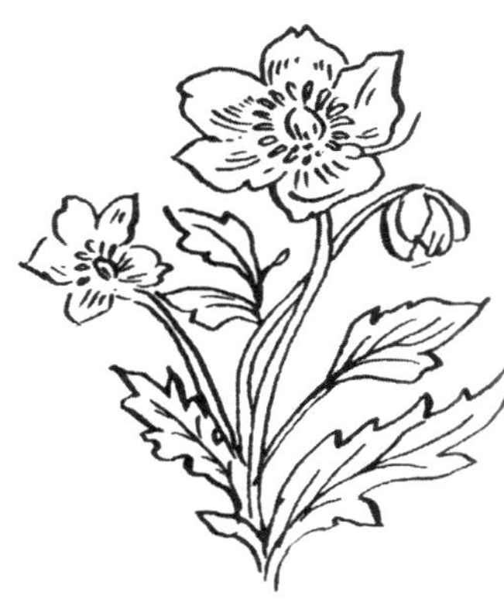

V. WOOD ANENOME

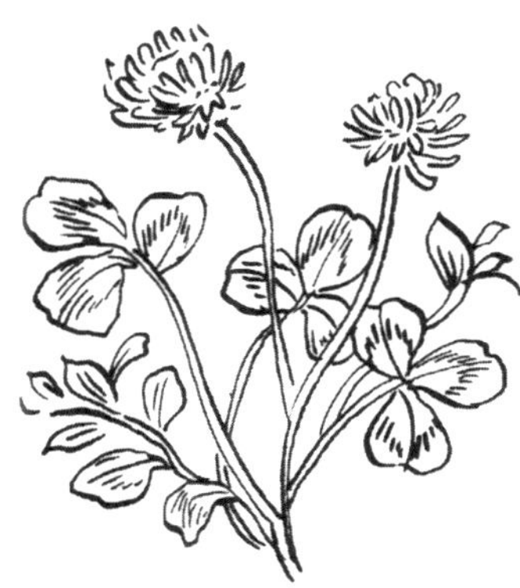

VI. WHITE CLOVER

VII. DOG ROSE

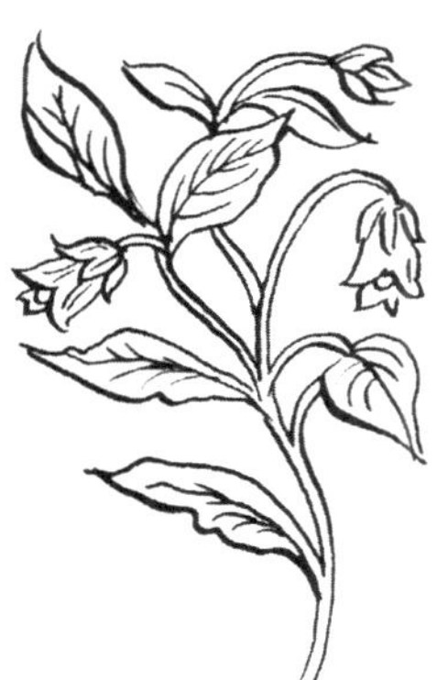

VIII. DEADLY NIGHTSHADE

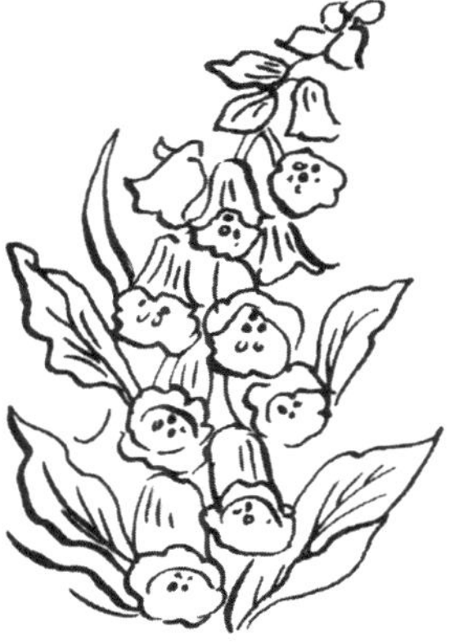

IX. FOXGLOVE

Woodland Flowers

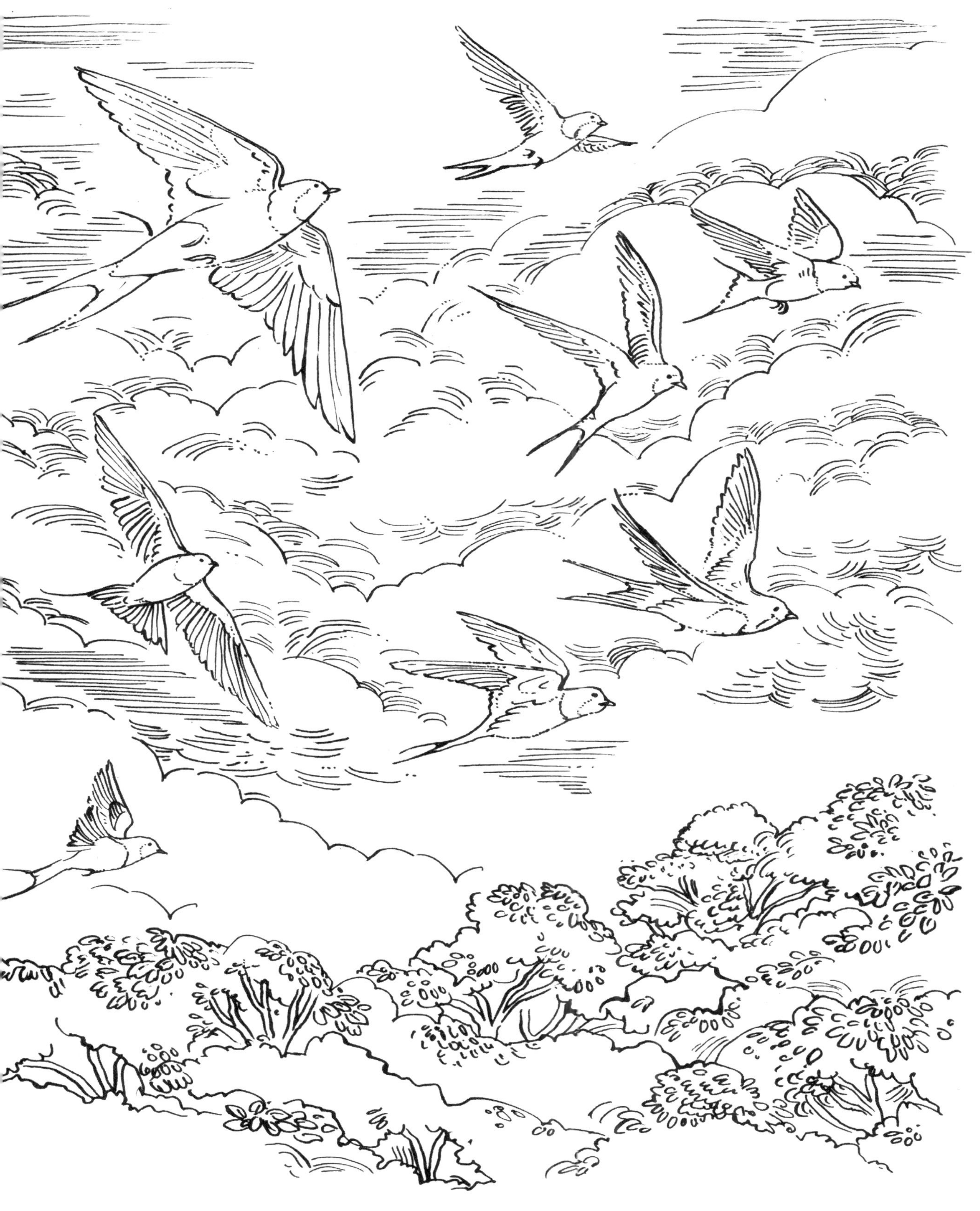

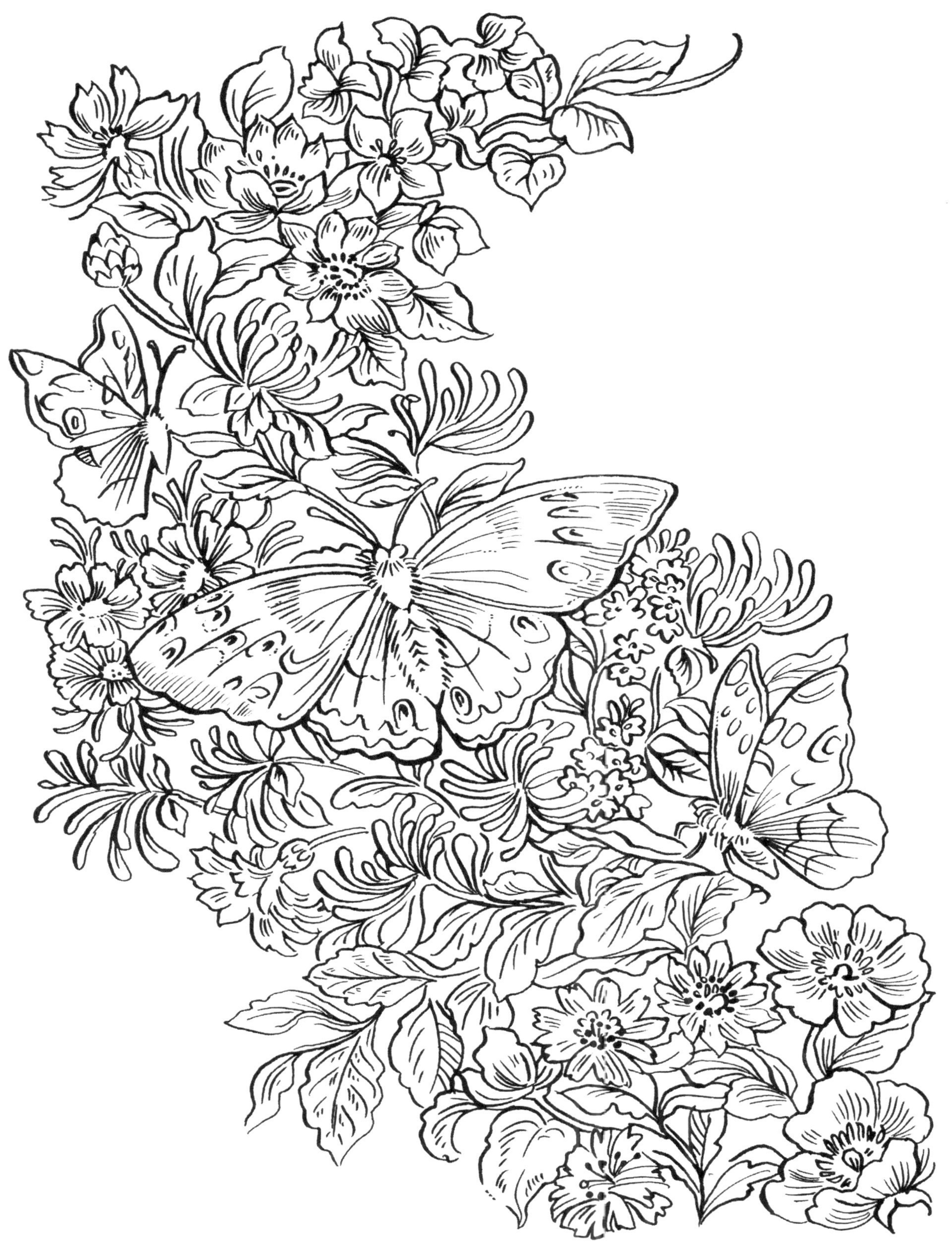

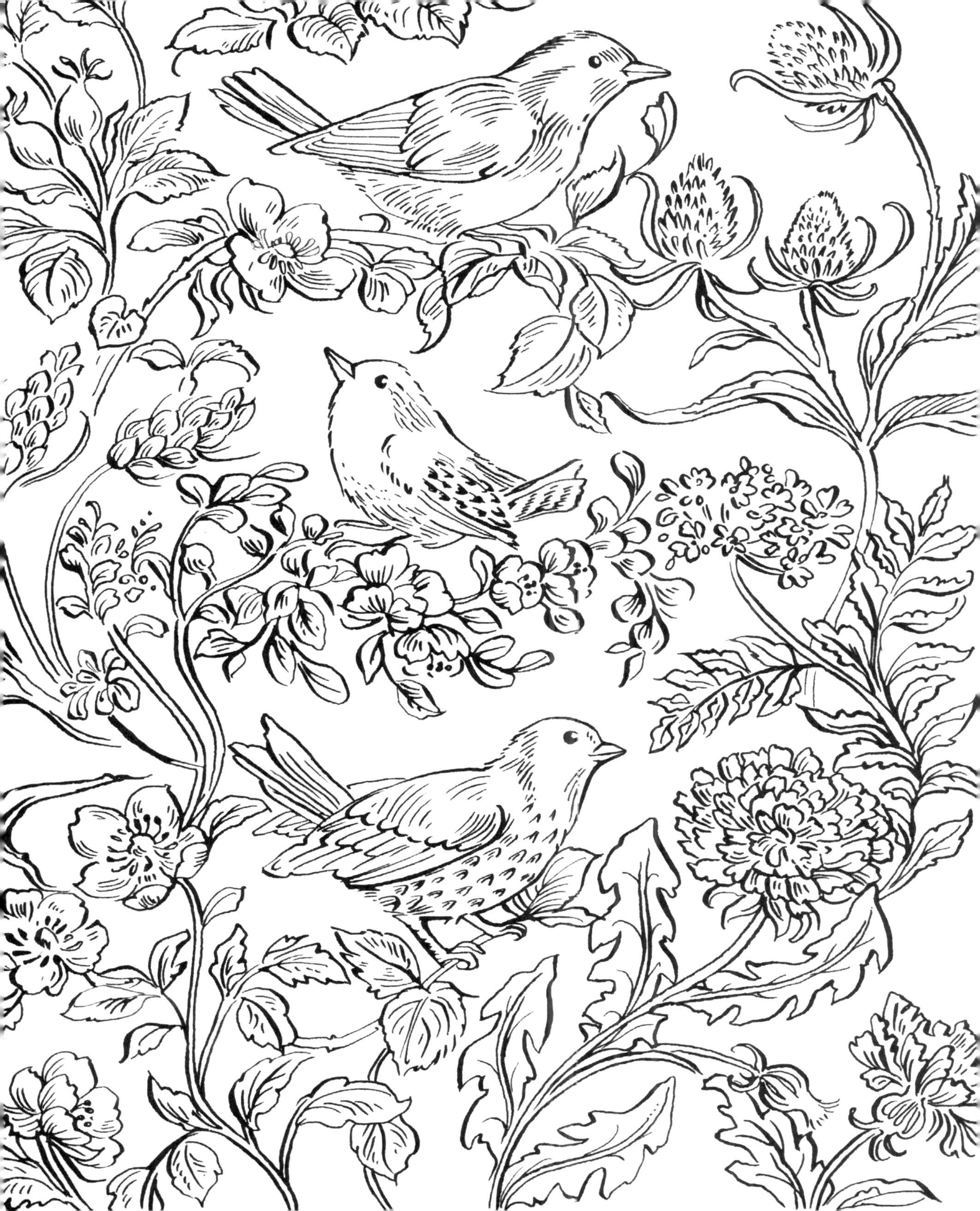

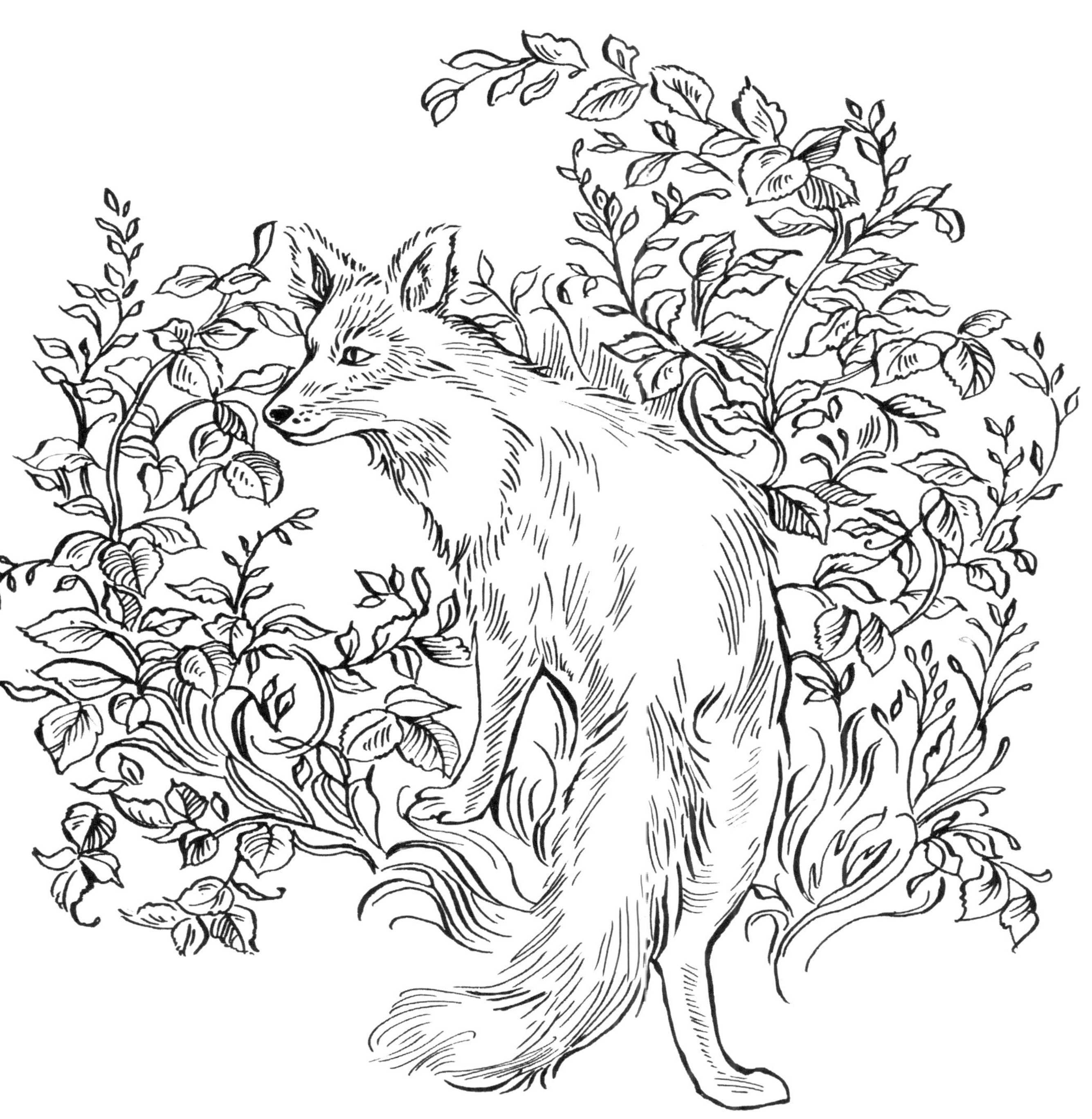

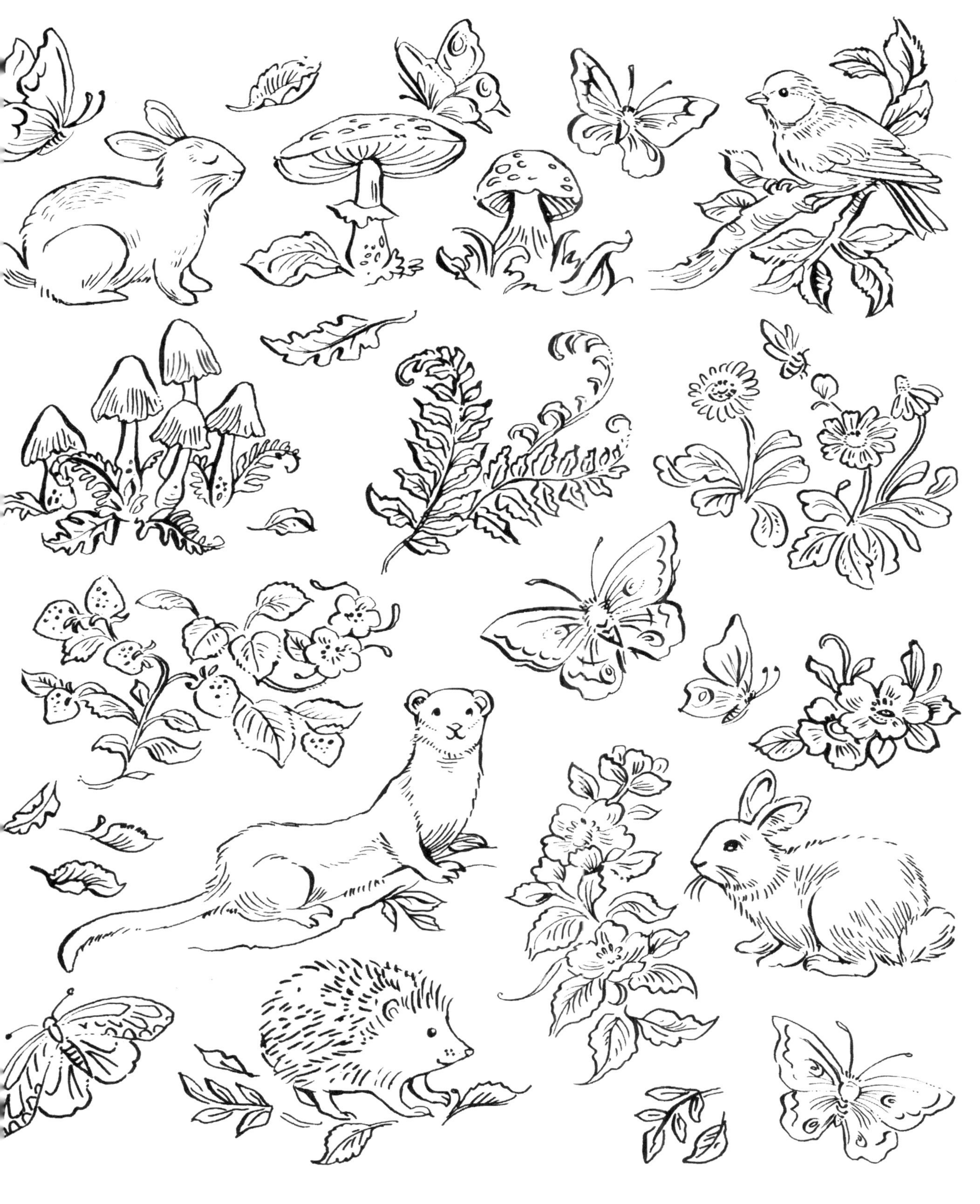

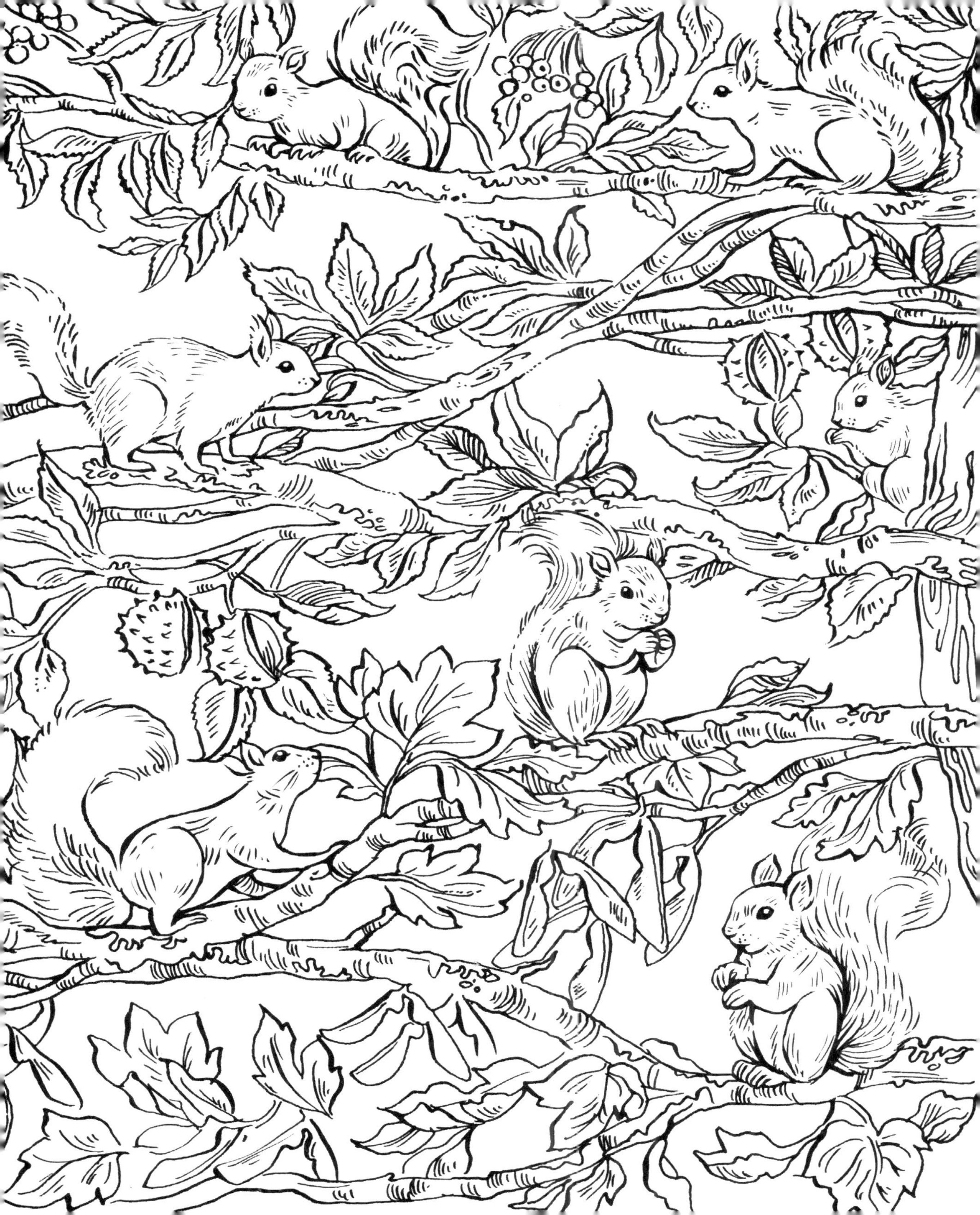

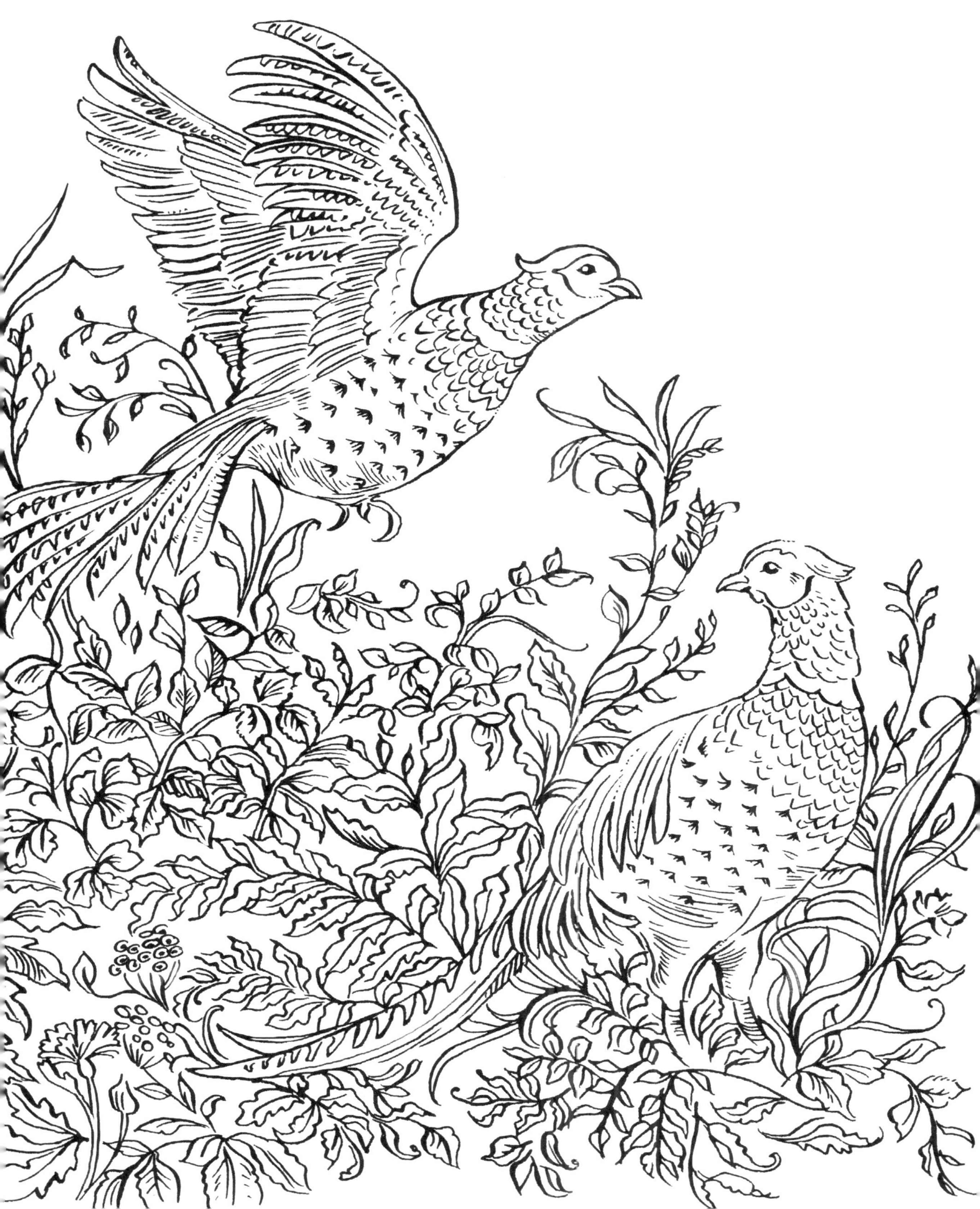

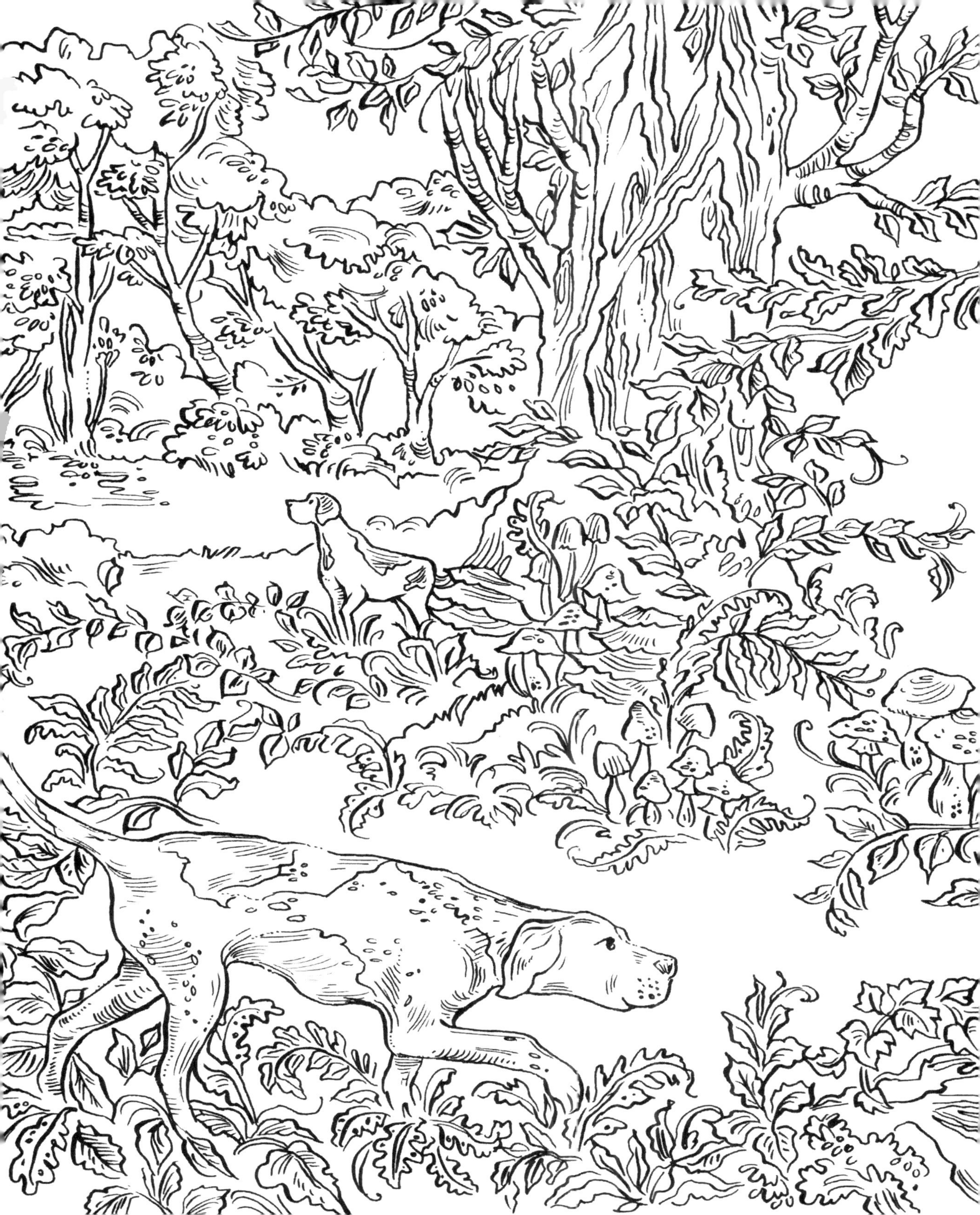

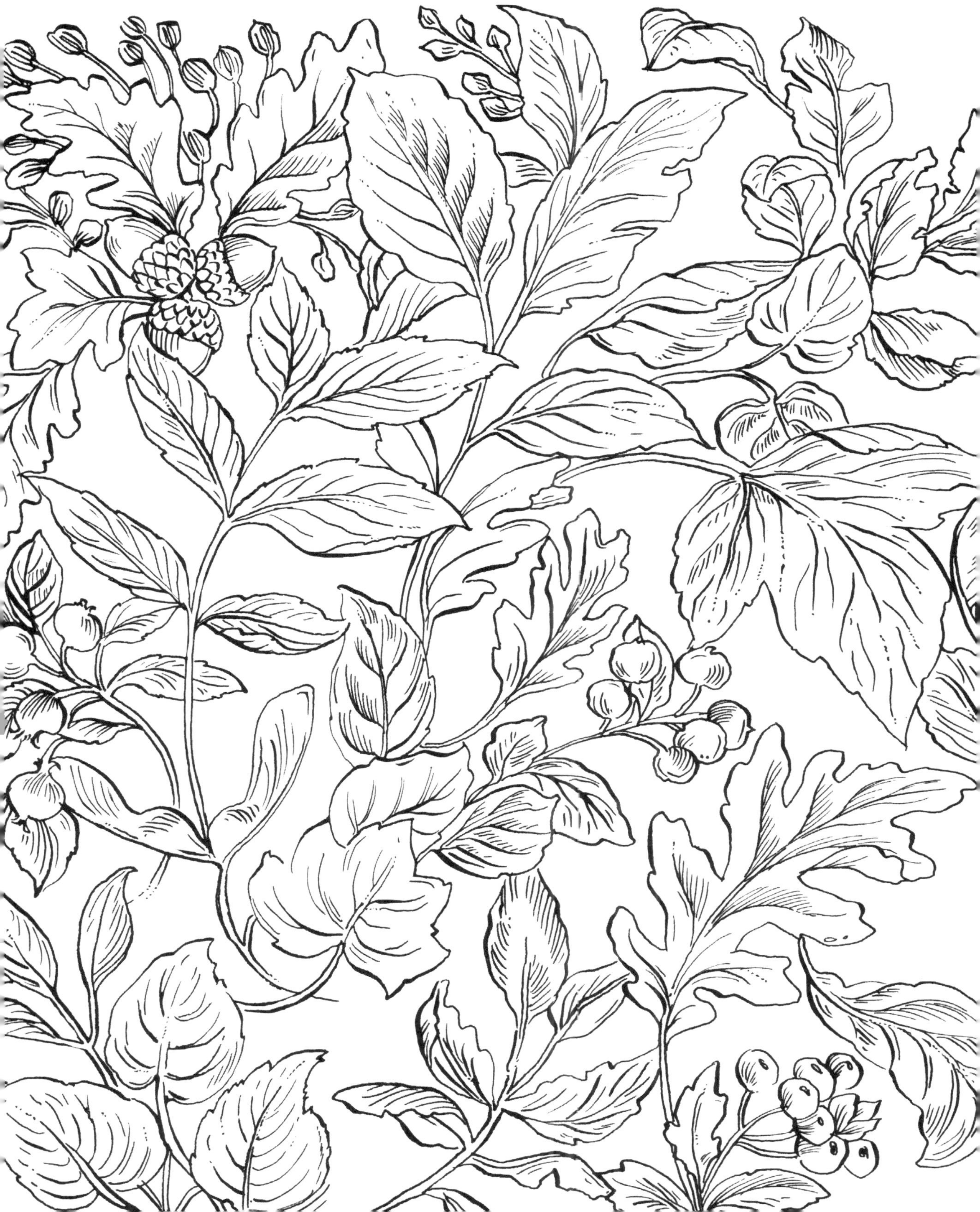

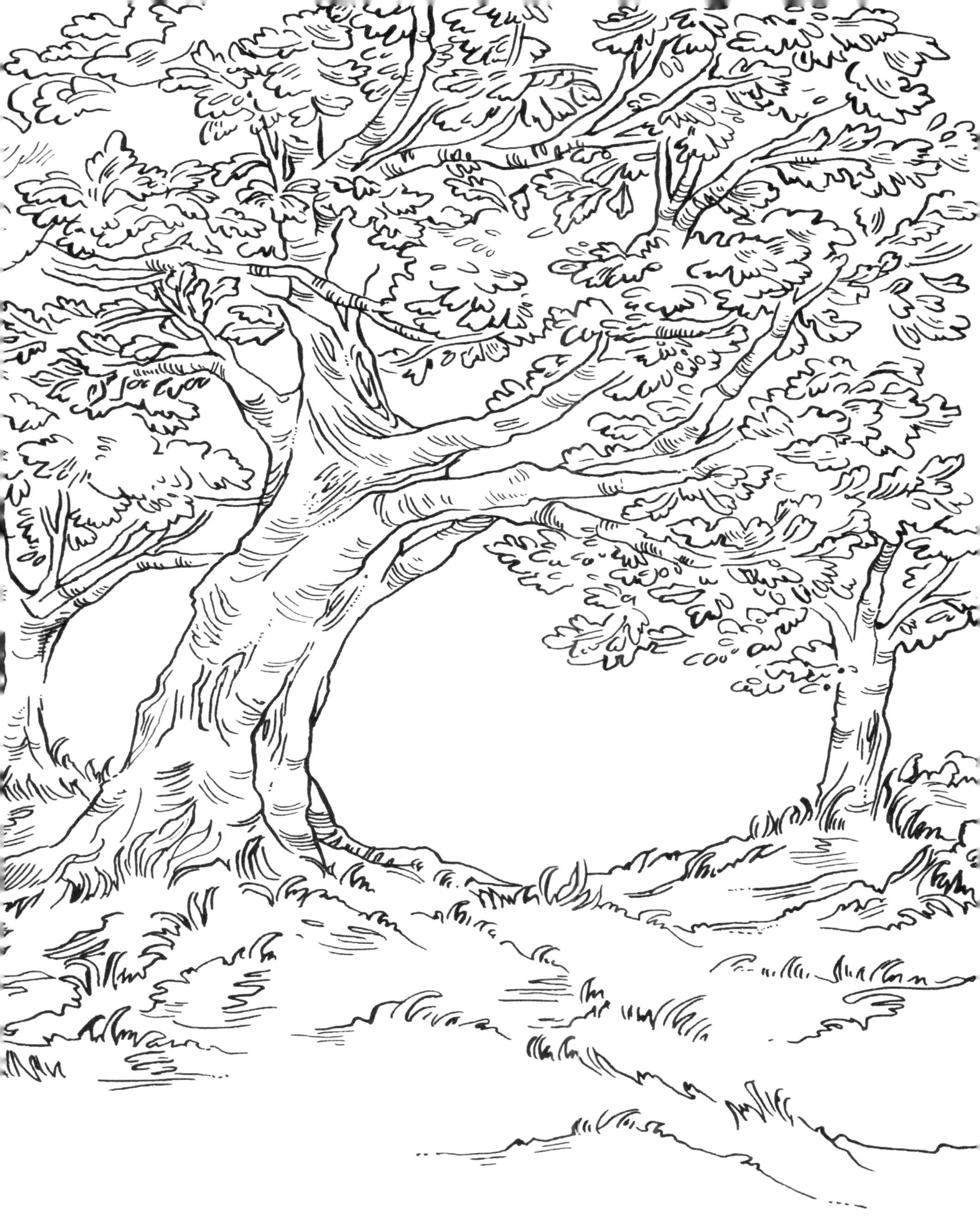

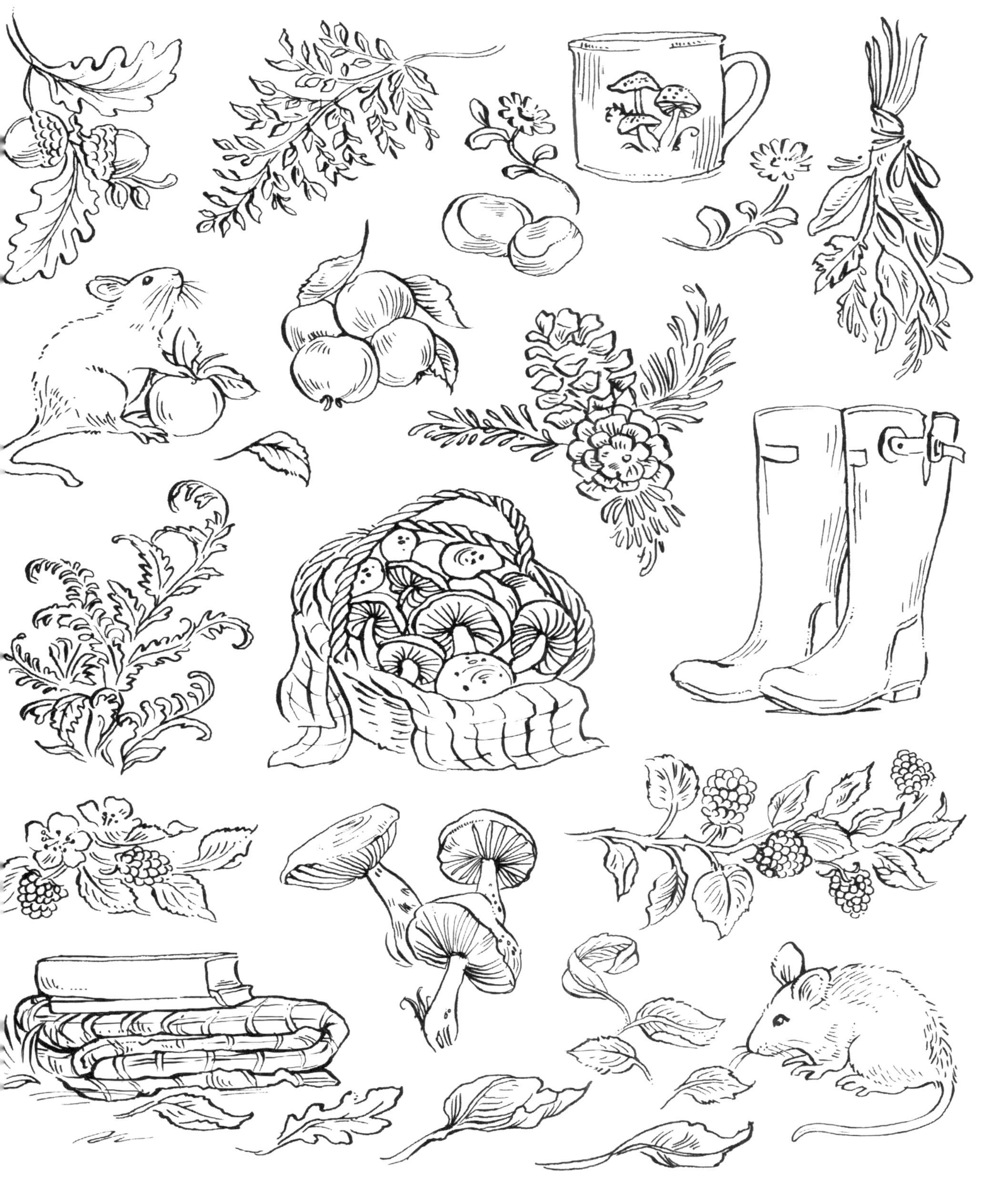

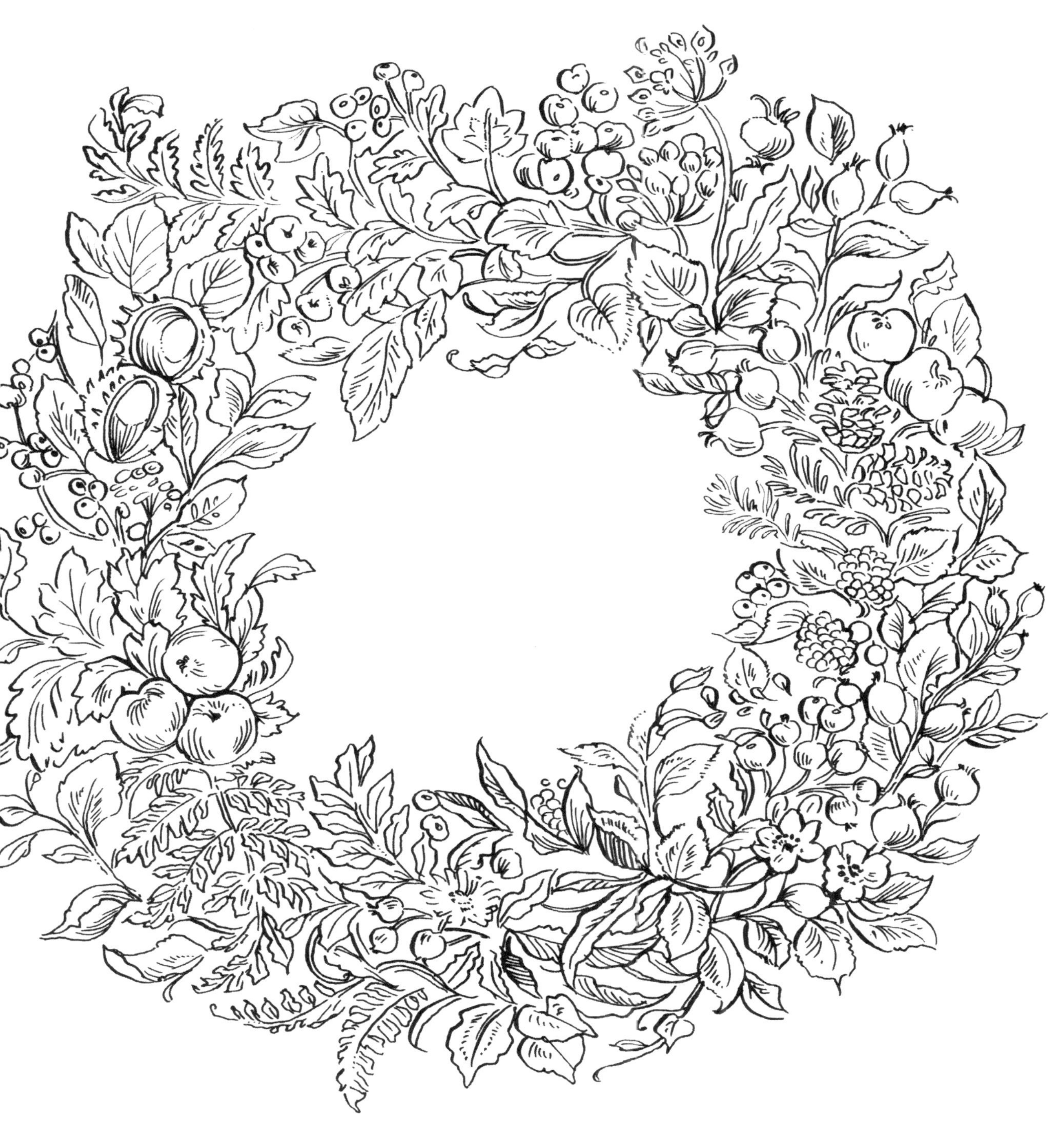

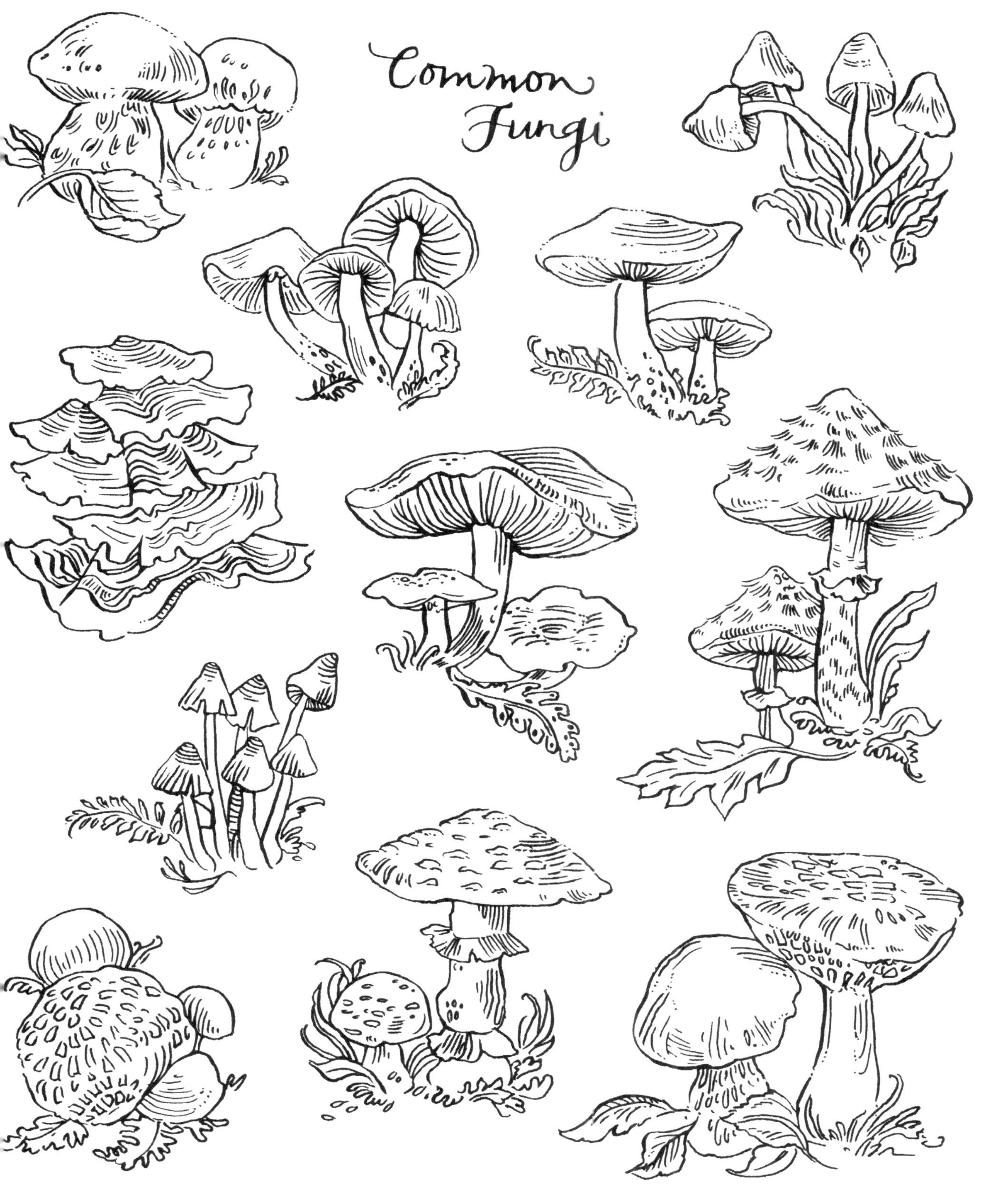
Common
Fungi

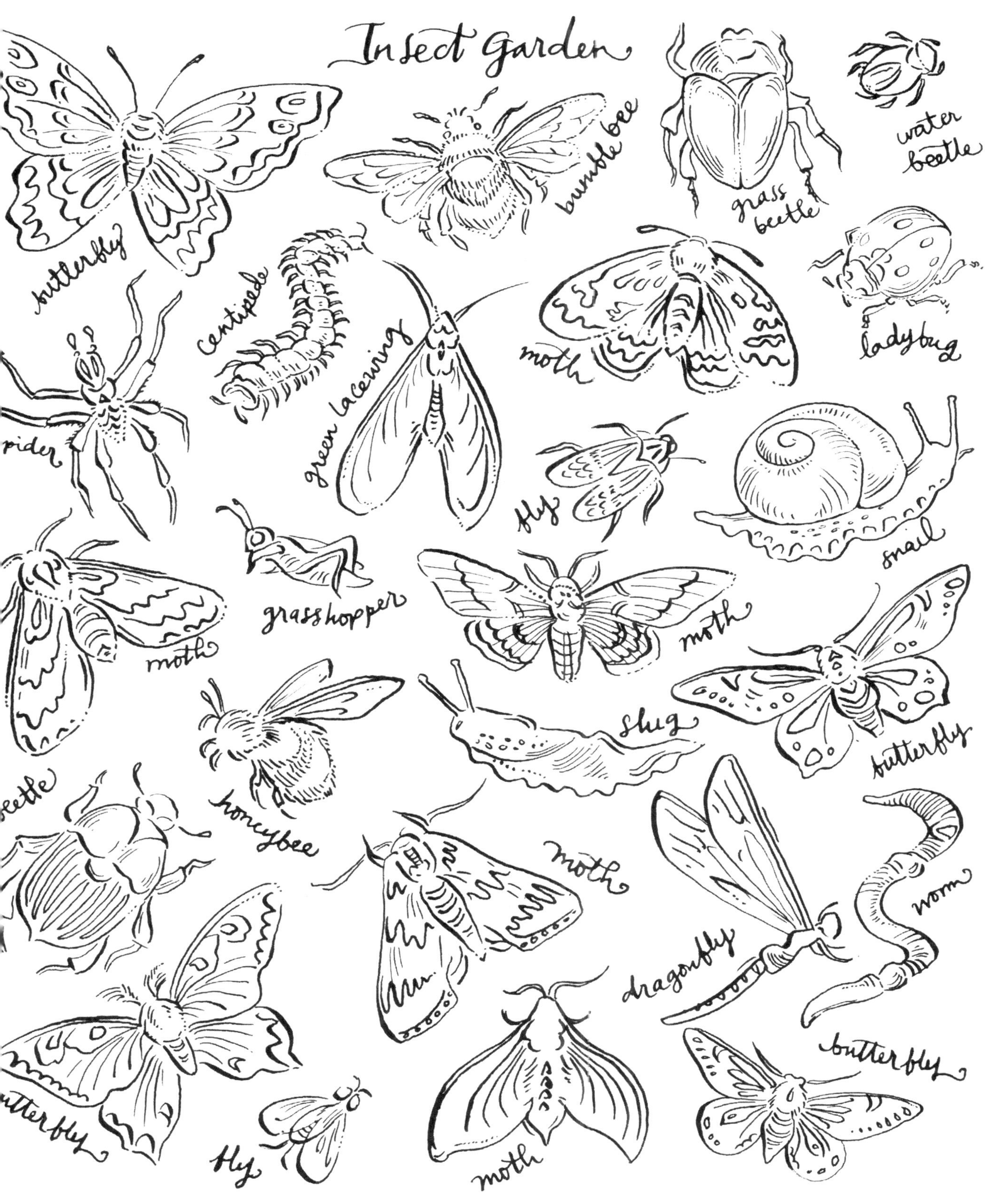

Insect Garden
butterfly
bumble bee
grass beetle
water beetle
ladybug
centipede
green lacewing
moth
spider
fly
snail
grasshopper
moth
moth
slug
butterfly
beetle
honeybee
moth
dragonfly
worm
butterfly
fly
moth
butterfly

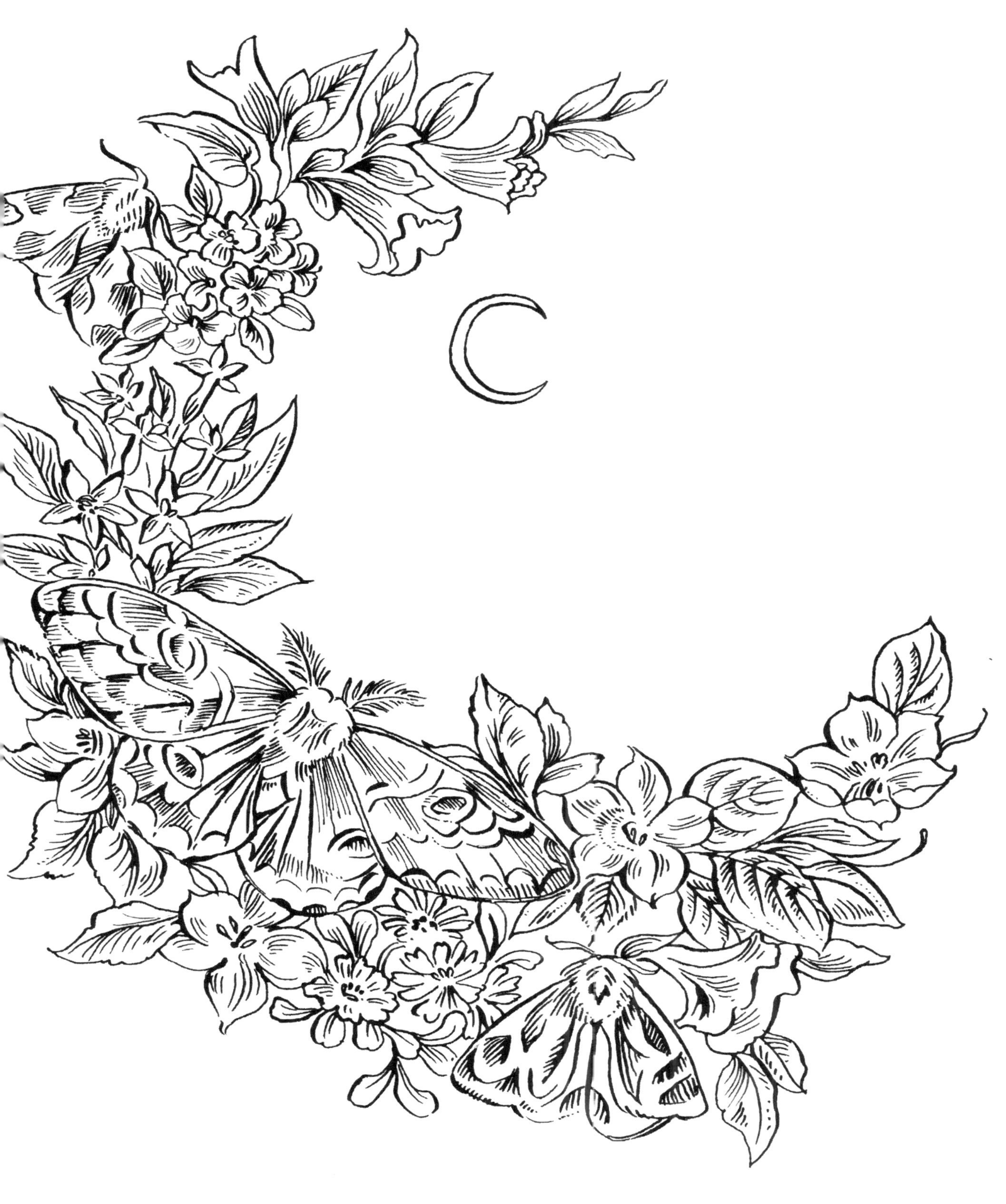

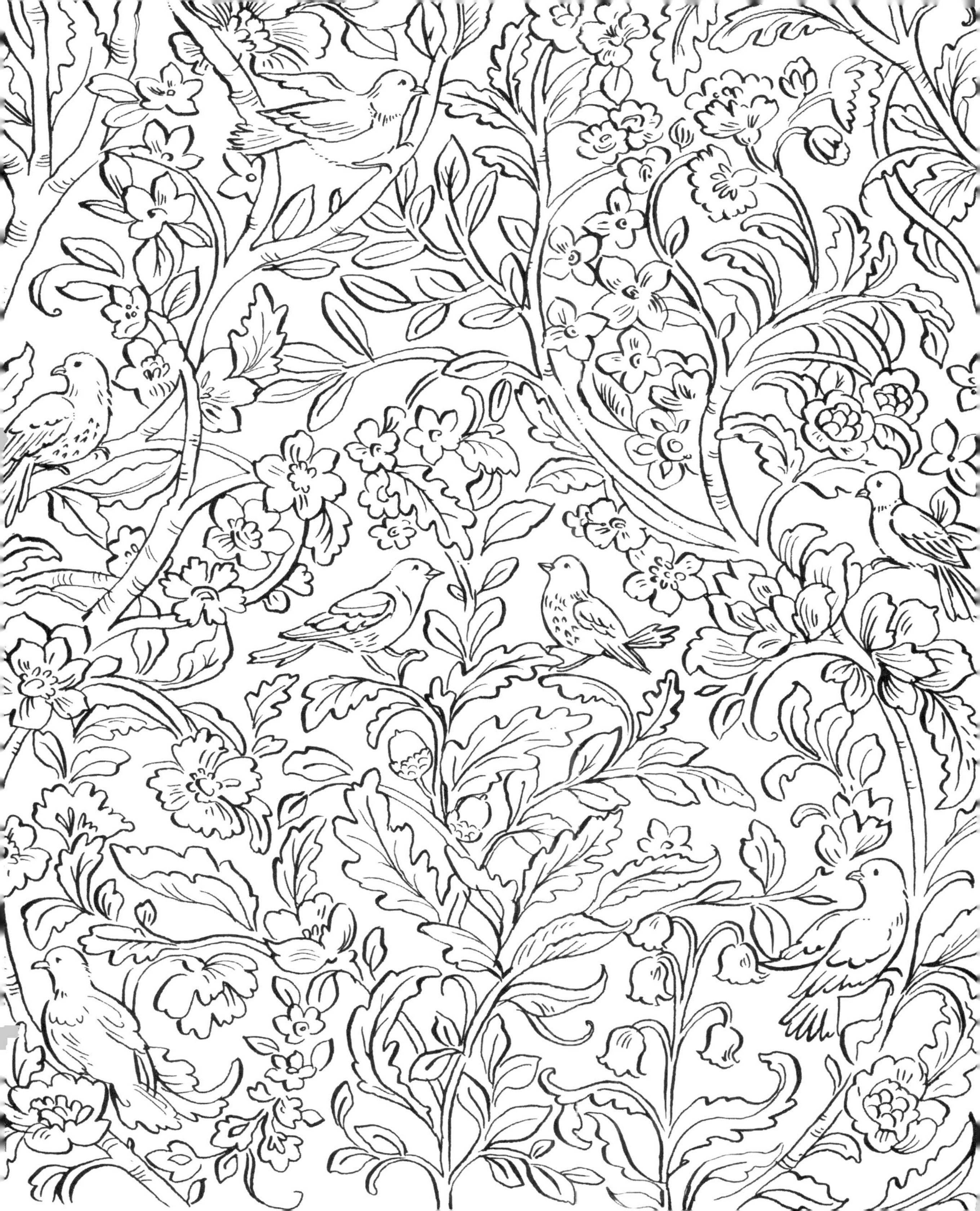

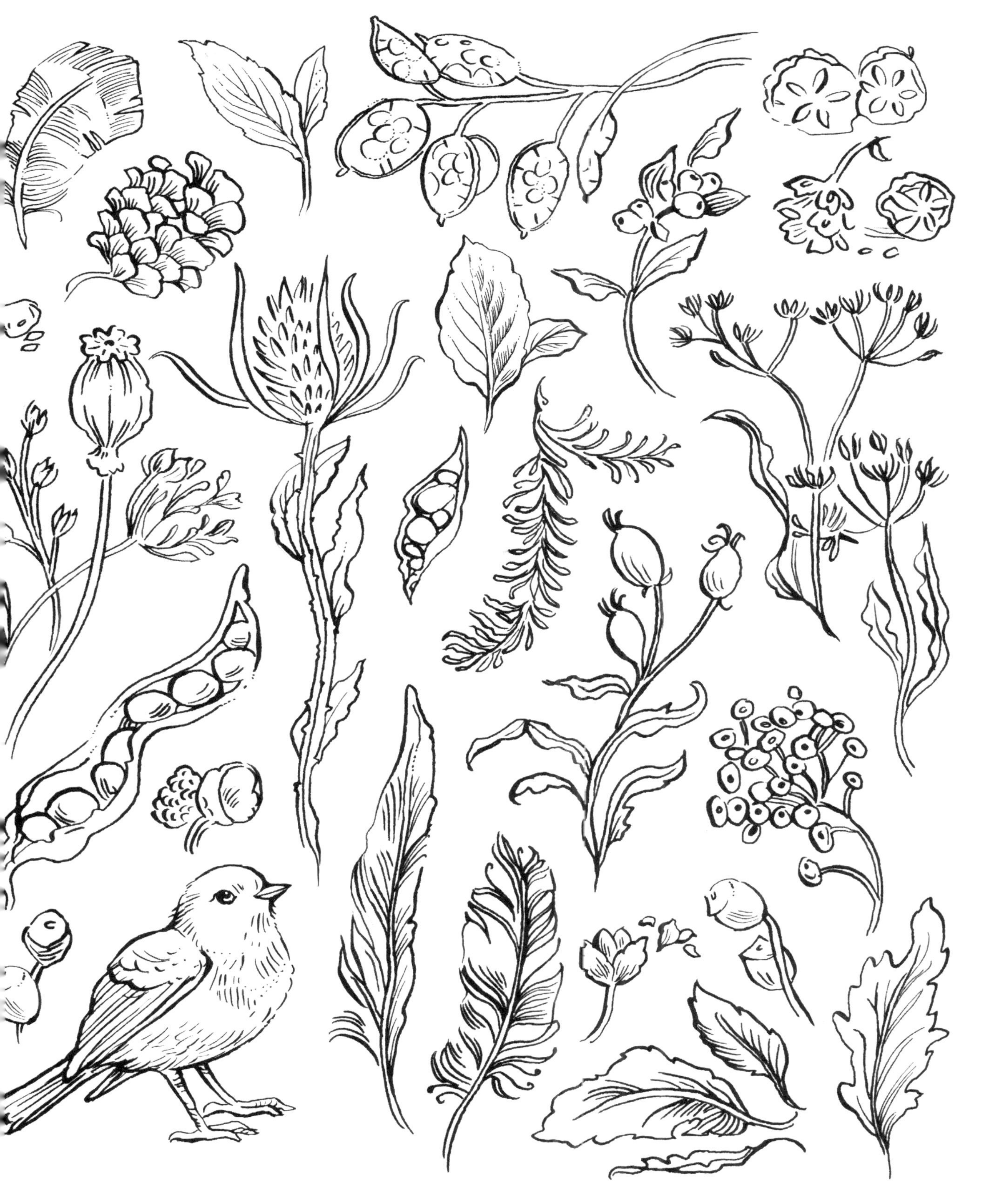

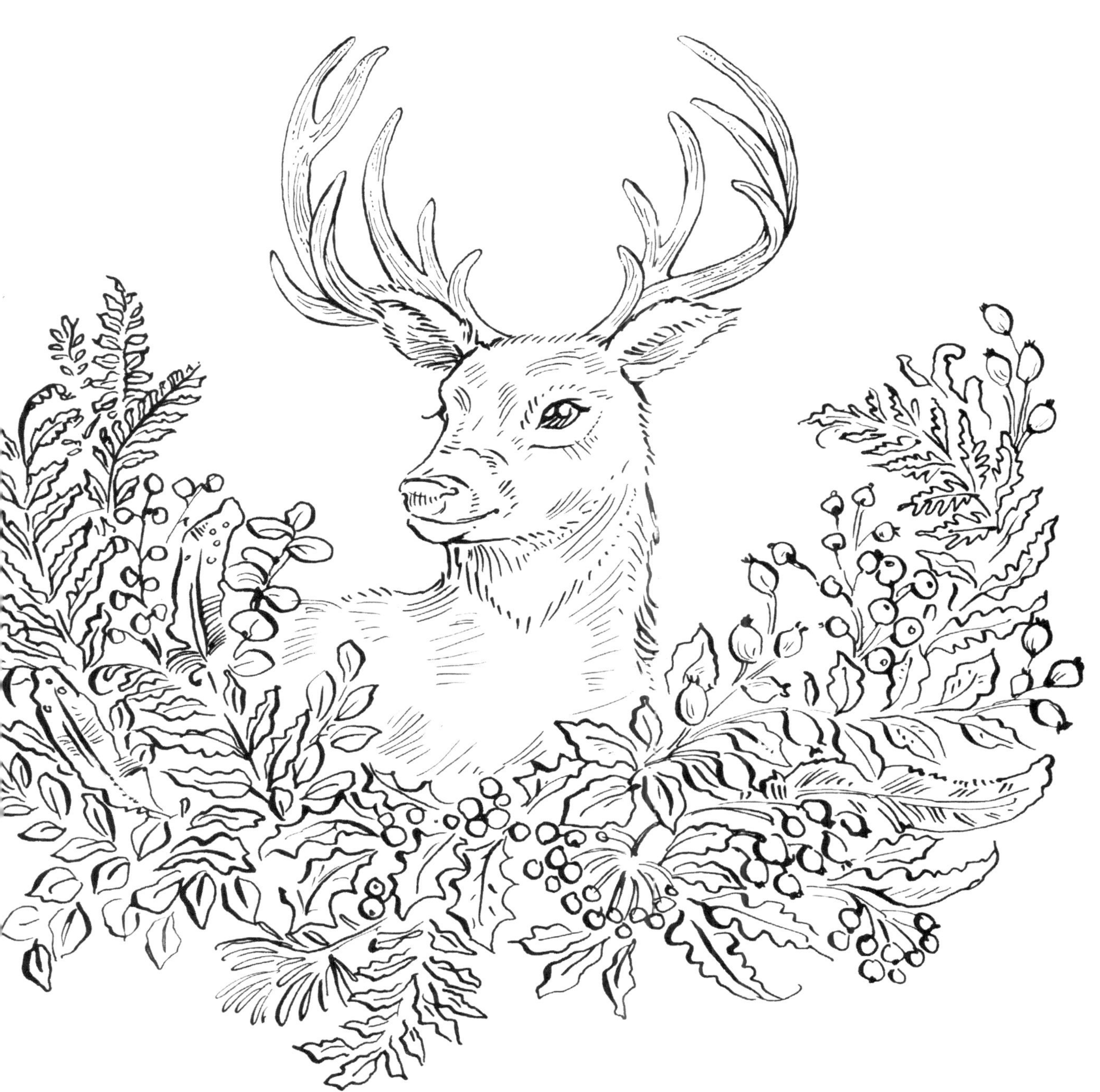

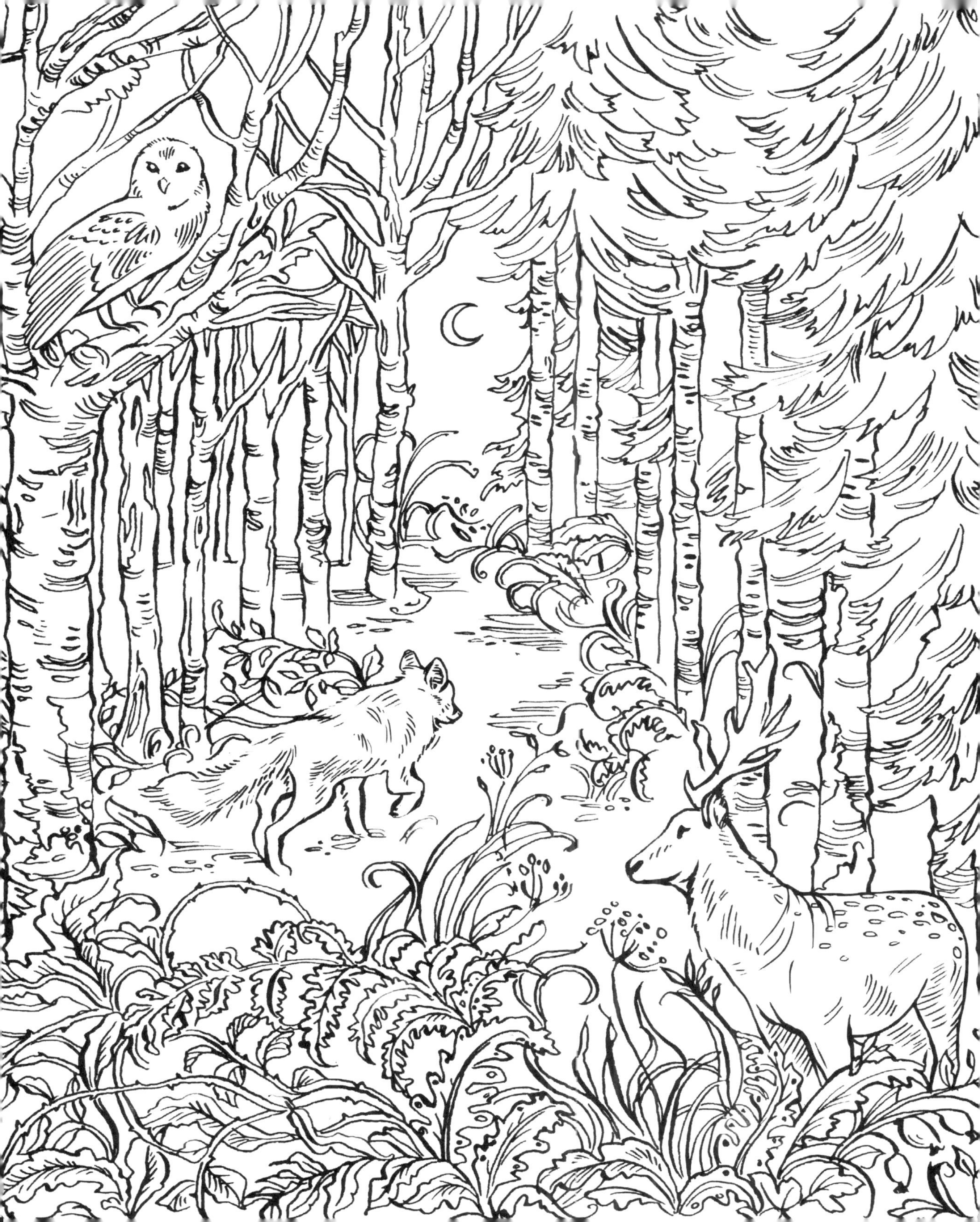

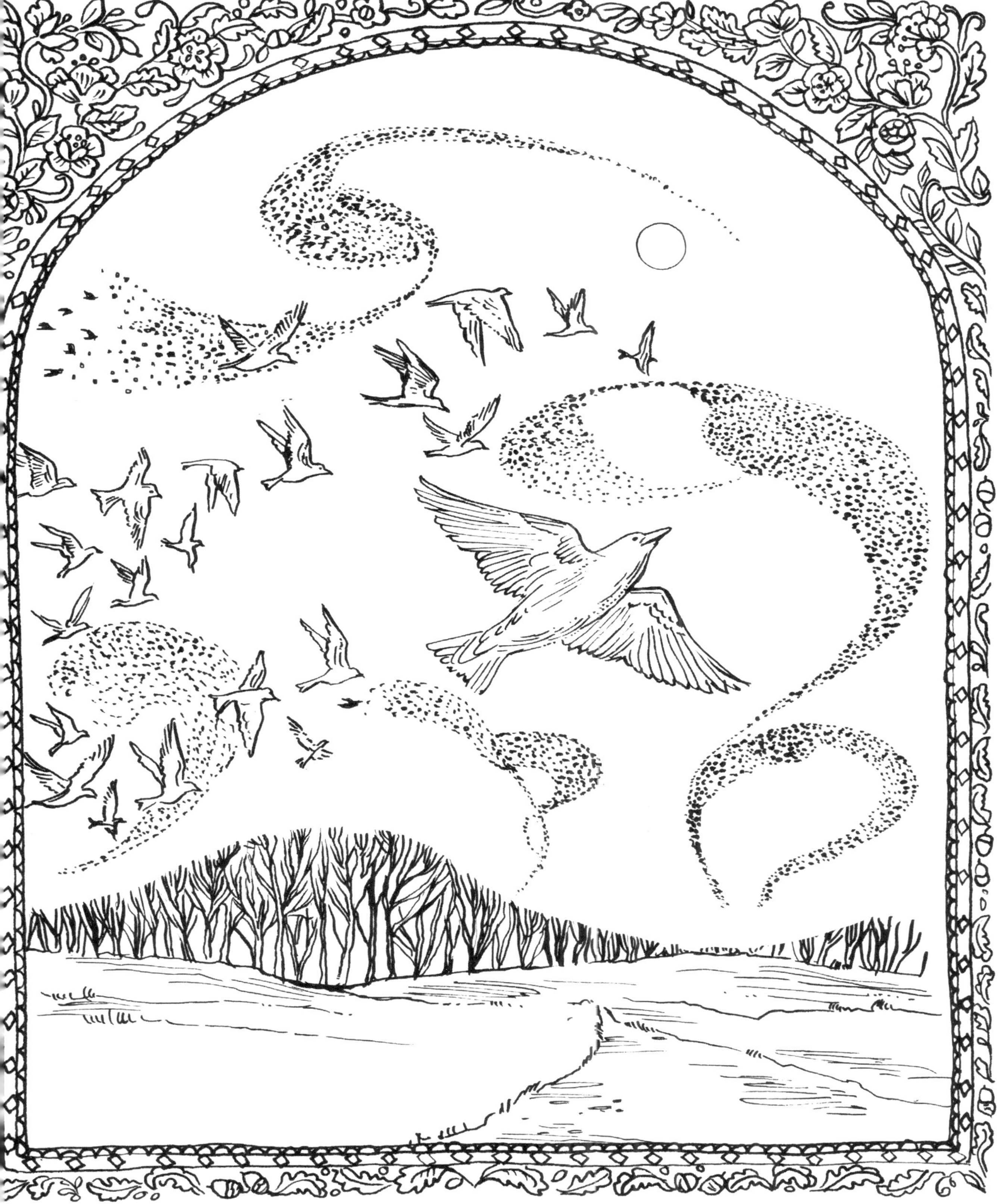

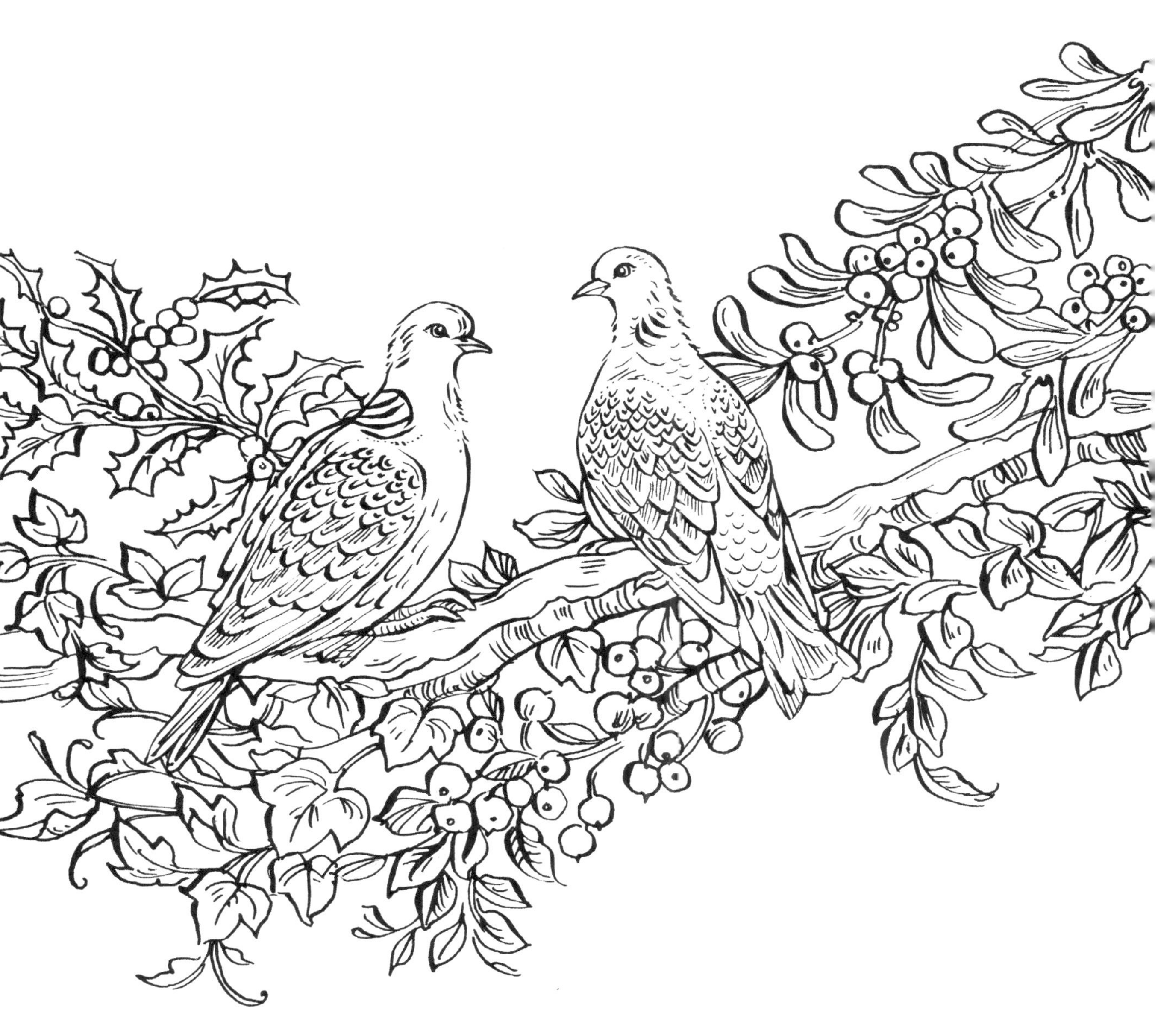

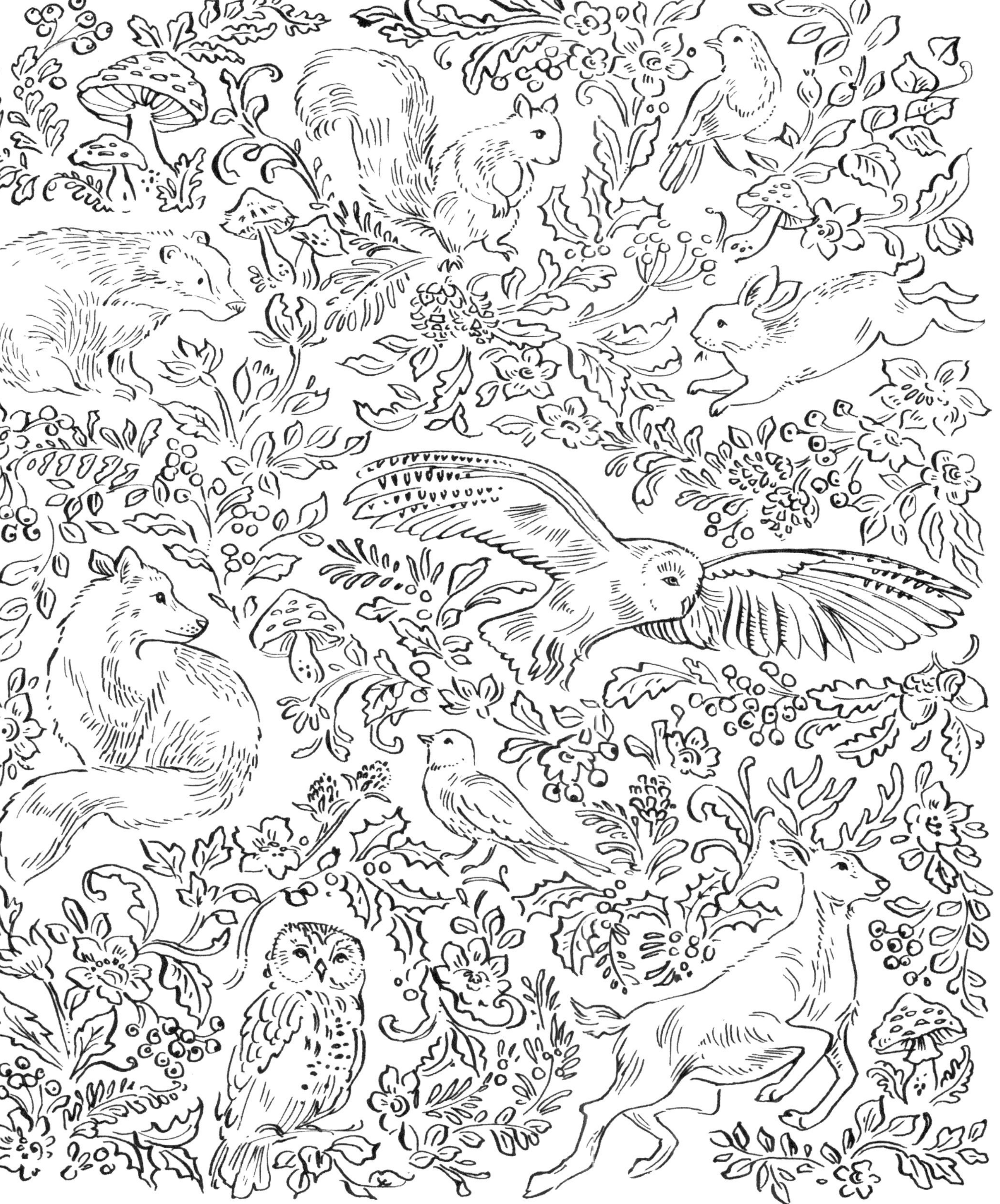

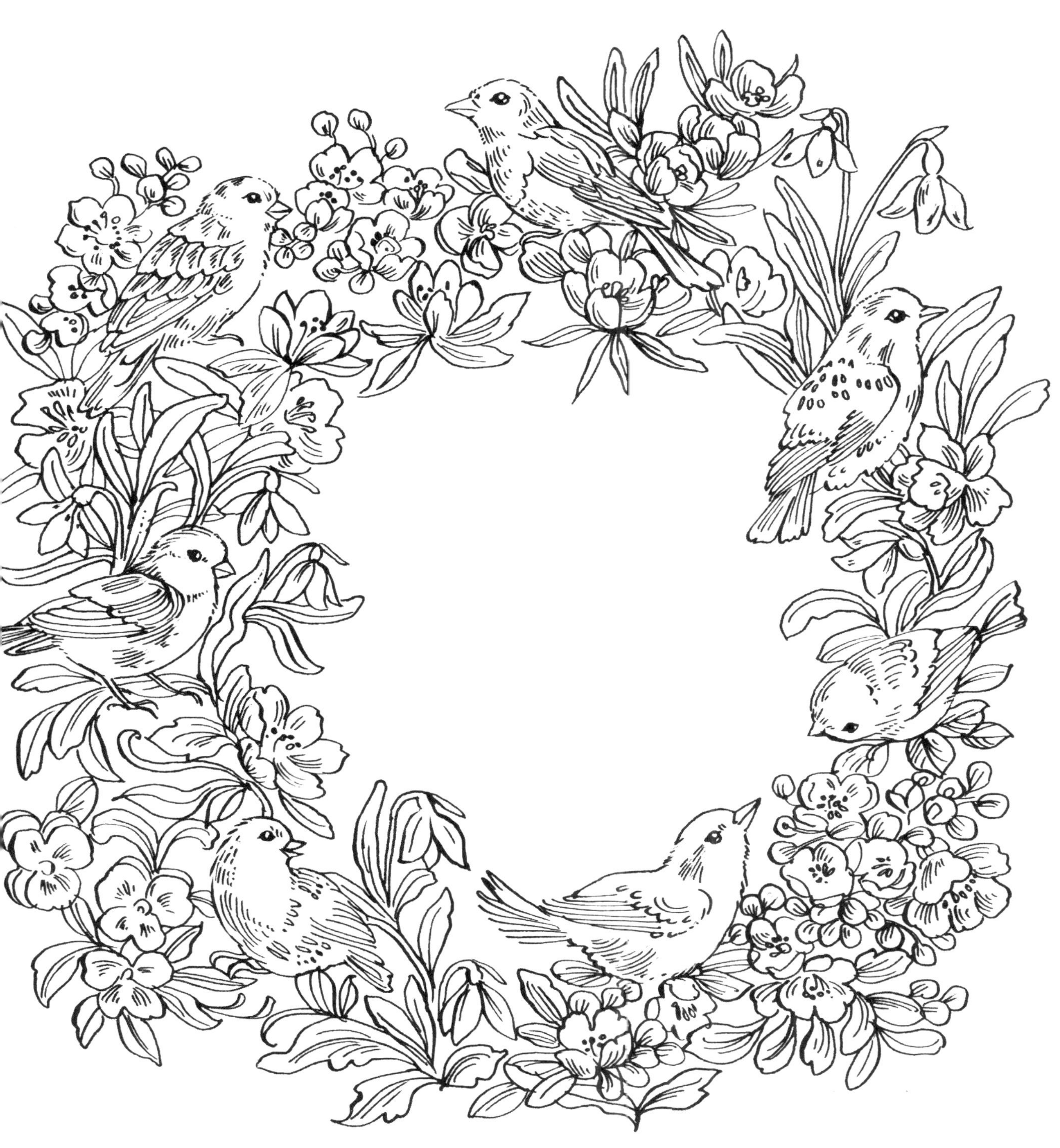

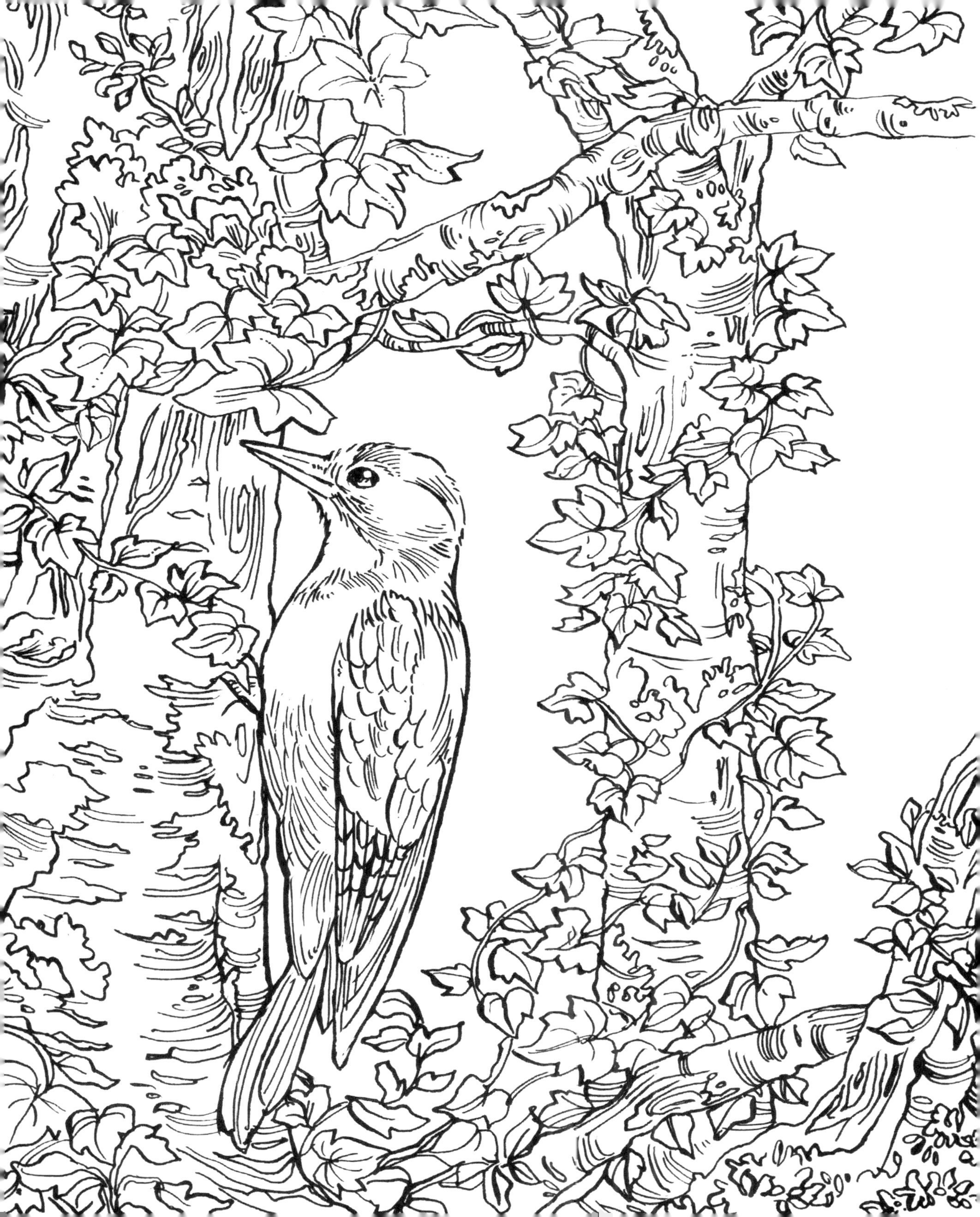

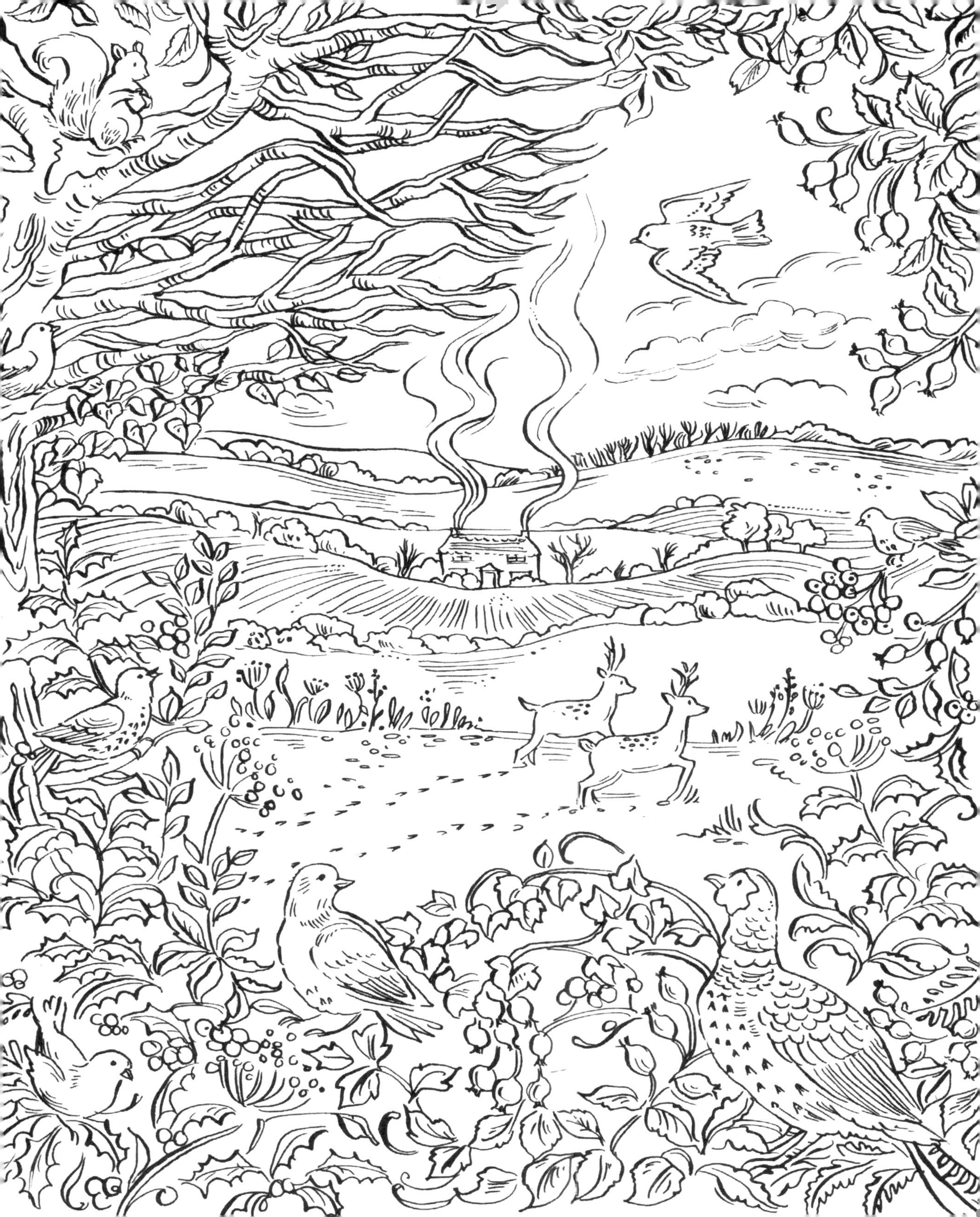